Beyond
CHECKS
— & —
HALOS

Beyond
CHECKS
— & —
HALOS

*Insights to Elevate Partnerships
and Achieve the Improbable*

Cynthia Eads Currence

Ripples Media

Published by Ripples Media
www.ripples.media

First printing 2025

Designed by Burtch Hunter Design

979-8-9921775-0-3 Paperback
979-8-9921775-1-0 Hardback
979-8-9921775-2-7 Ebook

CONTENTS

FOREWORD

Hala Moddelmog

FORMER PRESIDENT AND CEO, SUSAN G. KOMEN
FOR THE CURE, AND PRESENT PRESIDENT AND CEO,
WOODRUFF ARTS CENTER, ATLANTA, GEORGIA

Human beings are wired for relationships. Whether consciously or not, we seek out connections, conversations, and community.

I've spent more than 30 years in President and CEO roles at Church's Chicken, Arby's Restaurant Group, Susan G. Komen for the Cure, Metro Atlanta Chamber, and now at the Woodruff Arts Center in Atlanta. A truth that has resonated with me for decades is this: We need partnerships. We yearn for them in our neighborhoods, our businesses, and even our homes.

What excites me about this book is the way Cynthia dives deep into the importance of those connections—that partnership building—in the workplace and beyond. She gives us actionable to-dos and a fresh perspective that will transform the way we see partnerships in our world.

Cynthia shows us how businesses, commercial and nonprofit, can move beyond transactional relationships (if we even want to call a transactional relationship a "relationship" at all) and how meaningful partnerships can drive meaningful change.

I've worked in both the for-profit and nonprofit sectors for decades, and I've witnessed a huge shift in how these sectors relate to one another to cultivate partnerships. For-profit businesses understand now, more than ever, that "doing good" is good for business. Many in the workforce are imploring their employers to direct profits to change lives by improving communities, and businesses are looking to boost employee engagement and pride.

Years ago, many businesses viewed their philanthropic gifts without much strategic thought. Philanthropy was often just a monetary transaction. Without that critical, holistic understanding of the financial gift, though, its value was not as rich as it could have been. Today, I find that donors and corporate partners genuinely desire to understand who and what their investment impacts, whether that's children, art, or education. To add another layer, not only do these donors want to see their philanthropic impact, but they also want to understand any related local, national, or global issues. They're inquiring about the root causes of the issues. Why is our community facing food insecurity or poverty? Why are children lacking access to the arts? They're asking these comprehensive questions and seem eager to partner to create bold change that benefits the corporate bottom line as well as the selected cause.

From either side, the best way we can address these questions is through storytelling, which is what our Woodruff Arts Center Art Partners (Alliance Theatre, Atlanta Symphony Orchestra, and High Museum of Art) do best.

The beauty of this book is that it's comprised of stories that bring common business and community challenges to life. No matter your age, your background, or where you are in your career, I think you'll see some of yourself in these stories—the ones of failures, pivots, and silver linings. You'll likely see yourself in some of the mistakes that Cynthia recounts, too. I know I did. But most importantly, I hope you'll see yourself in the stories of bravery and bold connection.

Reading the stories of partnership in this book will uplift you and guide you, and maybe they will inspire you to forge your own improbable and lasting partnerships.

INTRODUCTION

This book is grounded in my passion for relationships that bring surprisingly powerful results. I especially love the evolution of relationships as people learn more about each other and begin to open up, trust, and explore. We don't always immediately see each other's superpowers or how we can achieve far more together than we can apart. This kind of conversation among people who feel comfortable with each other can lead to all manner of possibilities.

My appreciation for the power of relationships and the kind of communication that fuels them grew over time. Looking back, it might seem like a mishmash of knowledge and experience, but my journey was perfectly threaded with good timing and almost magical serendipity. I am amazed as I recollect the experiences that have shaped my choices and guided me to today.

I was a military brat who moved and started over every three years. What seemed painful at the time taught me valuable lessons about people, the fragility and resilience of friendships, emotional courage, and the blessing of opportunities to recreate myself with every transition. Travel also allowed me to study psychology at a Japanese university with students from

48 countries. You just don't stereotype groups of people from different parts of the world when one or more of them is in the room with you. They would set you straight. I learned that everyone is much more alike than they are different and that differences are important. In this uniqueness, we find new ideas that can enrich almost any topic.

We discern and leverage differences by listening with ears and eyes. That advice came from one of my Jesuit professors. He recommended that I practice quieting my mind so I could listen and observe better. To discover what that meant, I followed his recommendation to spend a week in silent practice at a Shinto temple. It is amazing what you notice when you stop talking. As I pondered what I learned there, I began to see how much I missed when I was talking or gearing up to speak. As wise people say, there is a reason your mouth closes and your ears don't. In silence, you can see yourself, others, and nature more clearly. This lesson has served me well throughout my career.

Continuing with serendipitous life events, this one springs from the basic need to eat in college. This led me to odd jobs, like teaching English to businessmen, working in a bakery, and modeling. Through modeling, I landed a gig as a weather broadcaster on the English TV station in Tokyo. This led to my working in a United Way pilot program focused on reducing criminal recidivism among juvenile delinquents. Serendipity! My psychology background qualified me to work with the kids, and since there wasn't a budget for a PR position, the bosses decided that my TV experience was sufficient to handle public relations.

I did well in PR not because I am a fast learner, but because of the power of networks. I had friends who were public relations and media experts. With their coaching and contacts, my United Way pilot program achieved 52 percent public awareness and favorability rankings over eighteen months—pretty cool for an intervention that had not previously existed. This success led me to become director of PR for Trident United Way in Charleston, S.C. Life was great, and luck served me well.

At United Way, I continued to learn from my mentors. Since I was focused on influencing public opinion and donor behavior, I also began to understand more about why people and companies would or would not support nonprofits. These early lessons are the foundation of many of my partnership successes.

First, I quickly learned to speak beyond the value of just "doing good" and to explore what was important to the prospective partner's leaders. For example, media companies survive on advertising dollars. United Way proved relevant to the media business because we had big advertisers on the board of directors, and we knew how to leverage their influence. Several of these advertisers gifted or shared space in some of their advertising buys with United Way. This distinguished United Way from other nonprofits with the media, establishing us as far more than a popular charity hungry for freebies. This business relationship with the media led to revenue and good public favor for both media companies and our nonprofit.

The results of this simple, need-based recipe delivered value to all parties and led to my next adventure. I was promoted to work as an internal consultant on communications and public relations for United Way of America. In this capacity, my ability to listen to what was important to others continued to sharpen, as did my passion for finding creative solutions with mutual benefit. After consulting internally for a few years, I was asked to lead communications and marketing for United Way of Greater Los Angeles, the second largest United Way entity in the country.

L.A. is where I attempted and failed at a large and politically complex partnership. We wanted to convince all three Los Angeles area television networks (yes, there were only three back in that day) to air the United Way campaign video at the same time. We involved our most influential volunteers and met several times with decision-makers. Unfortunately, we couldn't muster enough value to counter the competitive forces between the TV stations. This experience pushed me to relearn the lesson that bottom line value is king in negotiating with business partners. The reward has to be much greater than the risk, and the act of doing something good isn't enough value on its own.

Later, leading brand strategy and marketing for the American Cancer Society, I had enough money in my budget to hone my ability to listen by using formal market research. Qualitative and quantitative research is essential to understanding benefits and risks related to partnership concepts. Using the right data was the backbone of the most powerful partnerships my team built there. I'll detail these later.

Only by looking back on my career can I see a tapestry that was so much more than a string of unlikely events. These experiences shaped me for the future. They made it possible for me to lead teams effectively and to see the extraordinary possibilities that can emerge when companies and nonprofits work together strategically. I have discovered that creating collaborative action for good is my calling. Writing this book, then, is part of a personal promise to continue to contribute to making the world a better place.

I have over thirty years of leadership experience in nonprofit organizations. I am proud of my strong track record in creating partnerships that involve much more than your average transactional benefit to both nonprofit causes and corporations. I've had the honor of working with major international nonprofits, including United Way, the American Cancer Society, World Vision, and Children International. I am grateful to have led teams of extremely talented people who achieved multimillion dollar partnerships with global companies including Citibank, Glaxo Wellcome, General Mills, MetLife, Procter and Gamble, and Microsoft. The true value of these partnerships can't be summed up with a dollar figure alone. Such relationships impact all manner of business objectives. In this book, you'll read insights dealing with creating value exchanges across an array of common business needs, including pricing strategy, product and program development, market entry and expansion, and much more.

The partnership stories and insights shared here come from my own experience and from thirty-five interviews I conducted with other experts who represent both corporate and nonprofit perspectives. I am grateful for the generosity and wisdom they shared. They hail from an array of companies including Coca-Cola, Delta Air Lines, Unilever, and IBM, as well as consultancies like Cone, Inc. and For Momentum. The nonprofit perspectives come from many causes, including the World Wildlife

Fund, Save the Children, Catholic Relief Services, American Heart Association, and more.

Drawing from this wide array of perspectives, *Beyond Checks & Halos* offers lessons that can transform today's partner conversations. I invite you to look at your partnerships in new ways as you consider how relevant you are to your partners and how you can negotiate more value for everyone. Ask yourself if you are speaking the same language as your partner or if you understand the true motivation at the heart of those conversations. And another big one to think about: Are you getting proportional value for what you are bringing to the table?

Asking questions like these will allow you to see possibilities you may have missed before. In essence, broadening the way we think about partnering creates a pathway to deeper understanding. These understandings then reveal how to leverage each other's assets, business models, and market contexts. Relationships created from this awareness and blended with courageous conversation lead to a special appreciation for each other's assets. Plans and strategies based on this mutual appreciation generate far more good for both corporate entities and nonprofits.

The insights shared here, backed up by behind-the-scenes stories, demonstrate how many business opportunities and challenges can be addressed better by working with strategically-aligned partners. This requires that negotiating partners embrace a mindset that prioritizes how all stakeholders (including customers and beneficiaries) not only benefit and gain, but achieve proportional value for the assets they leverage together.

Partnerships based on trust with curiosity about each other's business needs can give rise to courageously transparent conversations, revealing interesting opportunities to help each other. Spiced up with a pure intent for mutual gain, this is the recipe for excelling in previously unimaginable ways with far more value for all stakeholders.

One other interesting phenomenon can emerge if partnerships are approached like this. The bigger visions that emerge using this pathway attract others, and the impact for all continues to morph into new types of value. Rarely are the huge wins that are sustained over time made up of only one company and one nonprofit acting strategically together. This kind of conversation can draw in other strategic partners, including local governments, other for-profit or nonprofit entities, and even political or religious organizations with similar objectives or common needs. Managed strategically, the additional players bring uniquely additive assets, capabilities, or perspectives, including global and local thinking. The United Nations emphasizes this point:

"The achievement of the 2030 Agenda for Sustainable Development and the Sustainable Development Goals require all hands on deck. It requires different sectors and actors working together in an integrated manner by pooling financial resources, knowledge and expertise. In our new development era with 17 intertwined Sustainable Development Goals and 169 associated targets as a blue-print for achieving the sustainable Future We Want, cross-sectorial and innovative multi-stakeholder partnerships will play a crucial role for getting us to where we need to be by the year 2030."

The UN 2030 Agenda and related reports speak to the complexity of solving big problems and the essential need to build multiplayer partnerships to do it.

To launch into how corporate and nonprofit partnerships can be spectacularly different from the norm, it is best to start with a description of what currently exists. Corporate support for nonprofit organizations covers a wide range of causes. Corporations have invested in everything from clean water, climate change, arts, education, economic development, politics, and health to a complex interplay of needs and outcomes, such as lifting children and families out of poverty and more. Trends tracked by companies like Cone, Inc. and For Momentum have correlated corporate good works to business success. Good corporate citizens almost always demonstrate strong threads of altruistic motivation championed by their leaders. If you have been involved in profit/nonprofit partnership work for very long, however, you've witnessed an enlightened self-interest running alongside corporate good intentions. Companies maintain a business perspective because they must realize a return on their investments in business strategies and tactics but also in their good works.

That said, corporate perceptions of value from partnering with nonprofits are still generally confined to positive consumer affinity, impact on buyer behavior, and stronger employee loyalty. Such good-will halos are valuable, but they are celebrated more enthusiastically when they correlate to a company's bottom line or a specific business challenge. I have witnessed companies realizing a positive impact on a range of other business opportunities, including pricing strategies, product innovation, market entry or expansion, tax issues, and others, that hit the bottom line more significantly than halos alone. This book focuses on accessing more of those rich impacts.

This isn't one-sided. Nonprofits who partner with companies as I describe in this book generate much more than a check. Nonprofits are businesses, and although they don't generally talk about pricing strategies and market access, they work with these issues, too. Strategic alliances with companies can also result in creative solutions for nonprofits' concerns. Additionally, such relationships can bring access to an array of powerful resources not always available to nonprofits. Such non-monetary corporate support can range from gifts of products like computers, medicines, and shoes to volunteer technical expertise from a company's employees. Corporate volunteers can help build houses and stuff school backpacks, but they can also help with marketing, advertising, IT support, and more. The right focal points and parameters in a relationship can impact a nonprofit's ability to transform a social condition. Feeding America's transformation after the successful pilot with Sam's Club is an example of this. More on that later.

Strategic alliances between profit and nonprofit entities can transcend all expectations and can evolve in unexpected ways. Hopefully, you can see more of these types of opportunities in your own work as you read the advice captured here. You'll be able to pause and reflect on your own situation at the end of each section. Use the breaks to think more deeply about a partner's needs, their language, and how you can courageously discuss pathways to address common business issues. Consider how you can elevate the conversation from a transactional discussion to a broad-based exploration of opportunity in the midst of complex circumstances. May your time thinking about how this applies to your world contribute to your own unforeseen and extraordinary outcomes.

Time for a story on creating extraordinary conversations. While working at the American Cancer Society (ACS) leading their brand strategy and corporate engagement efforts, I developed a huge appreciation for exploring needs beyond what was immediately being discussed. One experience drove that appreciation more than any other. I received a proposal for a simple, transactional exchange: $150,000 a year for a license agreement to use the ACS name and logo on a Citibank credit card. Beyond looking good, the bank wanted to boost card use. But was this a good deal? And, could there be more value for ACS? We agreed to test consumer response, which resulted in increasing the license fee to $15 million over five years with access to the bank's communication channels to spread cancer risk reduction information. The data enabled a conversation based on more facts. Continued good faith discussion broadened the focus well beyond a simple transaction.

This success and other similar successes are reflective of the national trends correlating cause marketing and consumer behavior. This broader data led me to believe then, as I do now, that corporate relationships could be and should be more than "a check for a halo." In order to fully realize the awesome possibilities of this research, those in the nonprofit space need to continue to hone business perspectives over beneficiary mind-sets. Specifically, nonprofits must clearly understand the worth of any of their assets or capabilities accessed in partnership. Nonprofits must look at themselves through investor eyes.

This book isn't intended to be a new framework for partnership-building. It is focused on unveiling a secret sauce that can be applied to any framework. To gain a better understanding of this sauce and how it is made, I studied available secondary data and then engaged in two waves of my own informal research. I conducted individual interviews to analyze common themes in successful partnerships. The first wave of interviews was done fifteen years ago with some of the companies I worked with while at the American Cancer Society. It gave me a sense of how well companies and nonprofits understood each other and what types of partnerships they believed were possible at that time.

The findings from this early research indicated that most corporate dollars given to charitable causes at that time were essentially transactional. Companies saw nonprofits as beneficiaries and gave little thought to possible synergies around a company's core business objectives. The rationale most often given for supporting a cause (36 percent of the responses) was, "It is the right thing to do," and the companies did so in the hope that their efforts would be appreciated by their customers. This response was followed by "someone in leadership was touched by the issue" (22 percent) and wanted to specifically impact that issue. I found it very interesting that only 32 percent of my corporate contacts believed that a nonprofit had the ability to significantly impact more complex corporate business objectives or challenges.

In summary, my early research showed that companies believed in the possibility of achieving a "halo effect" from supporting respected nonprofits focused on urgent or popular causes. Companies also felt positive customer and employee perceptions led to deeper loyalty and affinity for the companies. Further, they believed they could activate these good feelings and the behaviors that came from them through promotional activities. Only a few of the people I spoke with back then felt that nonprofits could in any way impact other business issues such as pricing strategies (8 percent), product development (14 percent), market research (18 percent) or product distribution (20 percent).

In 2023, I revisited my original questions with another set of company representatives and expanded the discussion to include nonprofit experts in partnerships. I am grateful to these generous individuals for sharing their corporate and nonprofit perspectives, along with their insights on partnership building. You can see a list of these experts in the acknowledgements section at the end of this book.

Looking at responses from the recent interviews, some results have significantly changed over the years, but much remains the same. The majority of relationships between profit and nonprofit entities are still transactional in nature. Most of these simple arrangements are based on exchanging money for a reputational boost. They are seeking customer and employee good will and loyalty, and it is working. That is a good thing. The interviews also revealed how significantly relationships between profit and nonprofit entities have continued to evolve beyond customer promotions and employee engagement.

From these expert perspectives and from my own experience,

the stories I share here go well beyond reputational value. They reveal impact on various business issues. The stories include an array of topics: affecting pricing strategies through the work of General Mills and the American Cancer Society, product repositioning through Unilever's relationship with Direct Relief, market share increase with Florida Department of Citrus and the American Cancer Society, galvanizing support for the good of all as in the City of Atlanta and the Homeless Mission, and more. You will read about multi-sector partnerships impacting critical needs, such as the local partnership between Children International, the Catholic Church, and local municipal government in Honduras. These stories offer invaluable guidance for those creating partnerships today.

The most commonly mentioned insights from the partnership experts are:

Business. Partnerships are truly all about business. Companies will invest more in nonprofit relationships if they predict a measurable impact on their bottom lines or a measurable impact on pain points that inhibit corporate growth. Nonprofits who speak and act from a business perspective will achieve greater business investment. Companies who look beyond a PR lens and understand the culture of nonprofits will find more opportunity for value.

Alignment. The more powerful the alignment of interests, the more powerful the impact for all parties. Time spent understanding each other's needs is the key to discovering powerful alignments.

Valuation. All parties must know the value of what they have that is of interest to the other party. Value is different in different situations. Knowing the value of your assets and capabilities allows you to negotiate proportional return for access to those assets.

Currency. Understanding the various motivations for working together and which of these currencies are dominant is critical. Money or just money is not always the only reason behind partner interest. Other motivations can include access to influencers, networks, or intellectual property. Interest can also center on any number of business-related strengths or weaknesses, including reputation, credibility, and expertise.

Trust. Always have the best interest of the other party in mind and show this with your actions more than your words. Demonstrating genuine concern for your partners builds trust which is foundational to great partnerships, and a determining factor regarding tolerance for risk and level of investment.

Courage. Be vulnerable. Share transparently about business objectives, pain points, and challenges. Exploratory conversations based on rich information about needs and motivations produce the best pathways to creative and powerful relationship plans.

Follow through. Don't agree to something you can't do. Disappointing your partner by failing to deliver what was promised is a sure way to terminate current agreements and eliminate you from future considerations. If anything changes your ability to fulfill expectations, communicate quickly and renegotiate your agreements.

Serendipity. When opportunities just fall your way by chance, recognize them, be thankful, and run with them. Chance takes many forms, such as an old friend landing a decision-maker position in a potential partner at just the right time or hearing a pivotal bit of information at an opportune moment.

Being it rather than doing it. The greatest fundraisers, sales persons, and partnership makers are people who live and breathe what they do. They don't just do a job 9-5. The essence of being wired for growing relationships is who they are.

Whether you come from a for-profit or nonprofit perspective, if you are alert to the common threads mentioned above, you can achieve mutual impact on critical business issues in significant ways. The impact can be on a wide range of important topics to profit and nonprofit entities, including supply chain systems, new product or service development, media reach, pricing, brand affinity, tax issues, political influence, product positioning and much more. With proper alignment of partner interests and assets, the potential is unlimited. Unfortunately, these topics are rarely explored.

Some of the common barriers to discussing and finding such focal points for working together include:

Weak awareness of nonprofit assets from a "for profit" perspective. Profits and nonprofits may not realize what superpowers nonprofits have that could influence corporate business objectives and ease pain points. The reverse is also true. Parties may not recognize the value of corporate assets that could be tapped to expand relevance or value to the collective good.

Weak valuation of nonprofit assets. Even if the parties believe that they can strategically impact business objectives, negotiating a fair deal is hard if you don't know your value. The deal previously mentioned between Citibank and the American Cancer Society went from $150,000 a year to $15 million over five years because they took the time to properly estimate the number of new credit card users and the value of these customers' purchasing behavior over time.

Communications challenges. For companies and nonprofits attempting to discuss business relationships, it can feel like they are not even speaking the same language. Remember the book *Men are from Mars and Women are from Venus*? In fact, they do speak different languages. Those who take the time to speak the other's language will succeed far more in negotiating. This effort builds trust, which opens channels for deeper conversations.

Negotiation skills. Nonprofits don't typically hire staff with business negotiation skills. They are at a disadvantage if their negotiator is someone with a beneficiary mindset rather than a business mindset. Companies can have costly blindspots, too. Those who see nonprofits as beneficiaries rather than business partners can make circumstances worse by discounting nonprofit input.

Knowing what currency to use. Figure out what really motivates your partner. Understanding what drives them helps you focus and become more relevant. The reasons for pursuing a relationship can be a complex mix of business objectives, money, reputation, influence, or social paybacks.

Ethical considerations. Corporations and nonprofits must be sensitive to the ethical considerations and perceptions of working together. Beyond adhering to regulations governing partnerships, this work needs to benefit the public at the end of the day. Companies should not exploit nonprofits for tangible or intangible business gains.

Weak familiarity with legal and tax regulations. Inappropriate partnerships that fly in the face of regulations can result in fines for all involved.

Shallow exploratory meetings. Preconceived notions regarding what parties have to offer and what they want from each other leave little room to discover greater opportunities. This point is evident in a story about The Coca-Cola Company and the World Wildlife Fund, which I'll talk about later. Essentially, their iconic partnership was made possible by deep conversations and asset mapping exercises. They moved from a position of neither really thinking they had synergy with the other to creating one of the most admired partnerships ever created.

The most remarkable stories I found are about relationships that went beyond the obvious or simple, transactional opportunity. The richer partnerships leverage all kinds of assets against mutually interlocking business challenges and opportunities. These are the relationships that bring significant and sometimes surprising value to all parties, including the customers, beneficiaries of charitable causes, governments, and the broader local/global community. Most importantly, the insights and advice shared here can enhance any partnership effort today.

My hope is that this book will help revitalize existing partnerships and help birth new ones that dramatically change the world for the better.

Beyond
CHECKS
— & —
HALOS

Chapter 1

———

MIND YOUR
BUSINESS

Great partnerships are all about business. There are many important factors related to partnership success, but coming to the table with a strong business perspective is imperative. It creates and maintains a path to huge gains for all involved. The importance of being oriented towards mutual business gain is not only a common element of my most successful experiences, it was a pervasive comment throughout the many expert interviews I conducted for this book.

Corporate readers may be nodding their heads in vigorous fashion when reflecting on the importance of a business approach. After all, their world is driven by business measures including revenue growth, profits and stockholder value. It can be frustrating for them if they are in a meeting where they seem to be the only ones wearing a full-on business hat. And, other nonproductive emotions can arise if corporate professionals are negatively judged for bringing their business smarts and their business self-interests to the table. Although it can be challenging, grounding partner discussion on anticipated business results for all parties with an expectation of business savviness is where richness lies for everyone.

Now, nonprofit readers, if you have begun to take even a slight offense, stay with me as I ask corporate readers to pause and let it sink in that nonprofits are also businesses. They may have a different language and their bottom lines differ from profit entities, but they are businesses. Larger nonprofits in particular are noted for a keen level of sophistication in business practices applied to their missions.

My point is that companies risk missing opportunities for phenomenal partnerships if they treat nonprofits like beneficiaries with inferior business acumen. Beneficiary positioning is dangerous to partnership building whether it resides in the heart and actions of a nonprofit or in the way a company sees and treats a nonprofit. This mindset undercuts possibilities and conversations that could surface unique opportunities for significant value exchange. And, as with unchecked judgments about companies, unmerited negative judgment of a nonprofit's business acumen can degrade respect and trust before you start exploring simple interests, much less something of bold potential value.

Keep in mind that first impressions are hard to shake. Once a nonprofit acts like a beneficiary rather than a knowledgeable business partner, they will likely be treated like a beneficiary from that point forward. If a company acts in a condescending manner or without the best interests of a nonprofit in mind, that sting will last a long time, too. This kind of unprofessional behavior, paired with any hint of disdain, is especially sure to end in a death spiral for partnership discussions.

What follows in this chapter are segments focusing on key business basics important to building powerful partnerships. They are laced with stories and examples to make the insights come alive. After each segment, you'll have a chance to reflect with a couple of summary questions.

Reflections

When have you witnessed a nonprofit acting like an "inferior" partner? How did that go?

When have you witnessed a partner discussion when both parties are appreciated for the value they bring to the table? How did that influence conversation?

MOVE FROM TRANSACTIONAL TO RELATIONAL

—

Most relationships between companies and nonprofits are transactional in nature. Transactions can be really good for both parties. They are generally simple exchanges of value that do not encourage deeper conversations about benefits beyond the given transaction. The majority of these straightforward arrangements involve an exchange of money from the company for some level of reputation or brand lift; checks for halos. For example, if a nonprofit is selling sponsorships to an event with a specified list of benefits and with no other objective for the relationship, this is transactional. Even if great people skills are employed with heartfelt appreciation, it is still transactional. It feels better when the exchange is stewarded thoughtfully. That said, this kind of exchange is still a beneficiary asking for a donation with fleeting positive exposure for the company. The same exact transaction will likely be pursued the following year.

To be relational, the parties must take the time to get to know each other with the intent to co-create long-term, multifaceted value for each other. They build an understanding of each other's business objectives, capabilities, and challenges. They share deep information to determine how they might complement or help each other. This knowledge is then used to create strategies that relate to specific business wins with measurable value to each party. Relational work requires regularly connecting and evaluating progress on those measures over time. The commitment to communication and targeted results allows relationships to evolve and, when necessary, to pivot based on any number of anticipated or unanticipated circumstances.

That said, relational work can be hard and doesn't always work out as one would hope. In the spirit of learning from challenges as well as successes, the following story demonstrates the difference in transactional and relational thinking in partner discussions. Doctors Without Borders (DWB) is a well-known organization that saves lives around the world. In addition to providing medical personnel in places that lack adequate medical resources, DWB also provides urgently-needed medical supplies. DWB's good reputation attracted the attention of Unilever, which was looking for a partner to help reposition their Vaseline product.

There was nothing wrong with the product. Vaseline was as good as it had always been, and there was no negative publicity around the product. The product had simply become a rather invisible staple item in anyone's medicine cabinet. Unknown to most who use it, Vaseline plays a critical role in medical treatment during disasters around the globe. The product's persona needed a refresh. Unilever believed that revitalizing the image of this common household item by showing its international superpowers would pull it out of the shadows of medicine cabinets everywhere and ultimately increase sales.

This is feeling like a transactional conversation isn't it? Stay with me.

Unilever didn't want a short-term series of events, stories, or news cycles or to create a momentary glow for the product. They wanted a long-term relationship where they could be part of good being done through use of the product. They wanted this goodness to be part of the transformation of the brand persona and promise for the product. To do this, the brand managers needed a partnership that would make a difference beyond the stories themselves. They wanted a partner that was able to creatively explore possibilities. In terms of assets, the Vaseline team didn't have access to much grant money. What they did have was pallets full of Vaseline. They envisioned starting the partner conversation around their ability to provide large quantities of Vaseline in exchange for emotionally moving stories about its use in disaster relief efforts. That initial core premise was a problem for DWB.

DWB didn't have the supply chain capacity to move the product to where it was needed. Its business model was to buy medical supplies locally. DWB needed money, not product. Aside from the fact that the Vaseline team didn't have much grant money, the deal DWB envisioned just didn't make sense from a business perspective to Unilever. The number of jars of Vaseline Unilever could give was far more valuable than what could be purchased with their available grant money. At the heart of the matter, DWB wanted a simple transaction based on their capabilities. In this situation, DWB did not come across like a potential business partner seeking long term, mutual value. They were perceived more like a beneficiary with a single-minded need. In this scenario, the parties' needs just didn't align. Beyond that, DWB was operating from a more transactional perspective, while Unilever sought a more relational approach.

There is nothing inherently wrong with transactional relationships. Such relationships create a great deal of good in the world. Focusing on simple, time-based exchanges of value can enable a company or a nonprofit to realize benefits without a deep investment of time and resources. With unrestricted money, DWB could move fast and get exactly what they needed by purchasing medical supplies locally.

Relational work is more complex and leads to more robust outcomes. One example is the American Cancer Society's (ACS) past relationship with Citibank. As I mentioned before, Citibank called me one day and offered to pay $150,000 a year for a license agreement to use the ACS logo and name on a credit card. This was a transactional request with some benefit to both parties. It started to turn relational when I admitted that I didn't know what the ACS brand was worth in that scenario and suggested we conduct research to make sure they didn't overpay or underpay for the agreement. The request made sense to Citibank, and they agreed to pay for research that we designed together. We agreed to base the cost of the licensing fee on the research findings.

"If one thinks beyond the halo for the company or the check for the nonprofit, there are powerful opportunities for all parties."

Ken Bernhardt Consultant and Regents Professor of Marketing Emeritus, Georgia State University

---

Citibank could have said, "No thanks. We want a simple transaction around a beloved brand and we know what we want to pay for it," but they didn't. They wanted to pay a fair price grounded in a sincere desire to make money while positively impacting the cause.

Our research focused on the response rate and activation rate from a small sample of the ACS donor base. The results stunned everyone. After calculating the business value based on this data, Citibank offered $15 million over five years to use ACS's marks. They also offered other benefits to ACS relating to the nonprofit's desire to better educate the public regarding cancer risk reduction. These benefits included specified access to Citibank communication channels, including bill inserts and newsletters. This relationship was founded on listening to each other's needs and working together to resolve concerns. This approach generated a long-term, multi-faceted partnership at a fair price with significant value for all.

Another story highlighting relational versus transactional behavior involves how Jane Turner led the Children's Museum of Atlanta. (She is now happily retired after serving as the organization's CEO for 18 years.) These insights are drawn from her partnership with the regional bank PNC. They center on building trust and friendship as a foundation to building a powerful and sustainable partnership.

When Pittsburgh-based PNC entered the Atlanta market, the company wanted to do more than just build awareness of their company. They wanted to build a solid reputation as a good corporate citizen in this new market. Concern for people in the markets where they work is part of the fabric of their values and key to the brand's persona. As such, PNC's philanthropic investments were inseparable from their business objectives. One focal point of their philanthropy was early childhood development and education.

As PNC made efforts to identify and meet influencers in Atlanta, they spoke with a prominent, civic-minded person, who happened to also be a big fan of the Children's Museum. She championed the nonprofit as one of the great options for demonstrating care for families and the local community. Her praise resulted in an unsolicited gift of $20,000 to the Children's Museum.

Jane was delighted to receive this unexpected gift from

PNC. As is her nature, she reached out to thank them and to get to know them better. She genuinely wanted to learn how she could support their efforts to contribute positively in Atlanta. This initial meeting set a tone of mutual concern and appreciation beyond the initial topics of gratitude and building up a civic reputation.

This wasn't a one-time meeting. Jane followed up regularly to stay current about the bank's business. She took time to ask about what was happening with them professionally and personally. She behaved like a concerned partner rather than a beneficiary jockeying for the next gift. PNC stayed apprised of how the Children's Museum was faring over time. Jane's ongoing outreach, without a second agenda, was the making of a foundation of trust, genuine concern, and respect. It created a relationship, not a set of transactions.

Not surprisingly, PNC's investment in the Children's Museum grew over time as Jane built multiple friendships with people in different positions at the bank. She tended these new connections with the same genuine concern. Knowing people well also helped Jane navigate the common disruptors of relationships (like staff turnover) with ease.

As Jane and her bank friends got to know each other's respective missions, needs, and aspirations, they discovered more ways to contribute to each other's success. This gradually unfolded in planned meetings but also in random lunches with the simple intent of staying connected. They knew each other as friends as well as professionals. This provided fertile ground for the natural co-creation of new programs and promotions with mutual benefit.

Co-creation is characteristic of high level partnering, a star we reach for but can fail to grasp because it requires comfort with fluidity, tolerance for risk, and a willingness to dive into unfamiliar topics. Guardrails are important when you co-create because the passion for the idea may lure you away from your core business. A quick side example of this danger comes from Children International. A beloved CI investor visited their programs in a developing country, and while there, he was struck by the need for access to clean water. CI's core programs focus on education, health, and economic development, not water. This donor believed that CI could and should incorporate water into their mission there. He and CI officials met several times to explore the idea. He went so far as to send $500,000 to start the effort. Unfortunately, it was a bridge too far for CI. They had no expertise in water, and diverting resources to start a water initiative would have resulted in negative impacts on their core programs. CI stood firm and returned the money with suggestions for other nonprofits that could address his passion for clean water access. This funder still supports CI, and his respect for their programs and their leadership has grown immensely thanks to the way they handled this exchange.

The Children's Museum saw a different outcome from co-creation efforts, which was helped along by a little serendipity. One of their board members recommended that they create a golf event primarily to raise more money. Golf tournaments take time to mature into great fundraisers, even with experienced staff. With no funds to carry the event-planning learning curve and no staff expertise or time to pull it off, it would have been natural to throttle that idea before too many people grew attached. This idea had all the trappings of pulling the organization off course. To honor those who loved the concept, Jane shared it, warts and all, with PNC during one of her catch-up visits. This is where serendipity comes into play. (Remember that word, you'll hear it again!) It just so happened that PNC was looking for such an event to boost their number of high-end bank clients. They had seen golf events work well for their competitors. Moreover, they loved the idea of playing the most prominent role in the event. They invested heavily to secure top-notch expertise. The tournament ultimately generated over $2 million for the Children's Museum and was valuable to the bank, too. This would not have happened if the Children's Museum CEO had not established trust and been willing to explore an idea well outside their wheelhouse.

Co-creation goes both ways. This story emerged from the same fertile ground of trust and openness, but this time, PNC initiated the conversation. The corporate headquarters team wanted to pilot innovative language development programs in key cities like Atlanta. The goal was to address the vocabulary gap in young children from underprivileged backgrounds and to help give these children a stronger start in school. Ultimately, kids with this opportunity would become productive adults and potentially great customers. PNC's corporate social responsibility lead reached out to the Children's Museum to invite them to participate.

Unfortunately, there was a problem. The Museum was focused on children, but it didn't do the intervention work that the bank wanted. Rather than try to force a fit, the Museum invited the Atlanta Speech School to join in a three-way partnership. Together, the nonprofits were a strong match for the bank's vision and were awarded $1 million. Perhaps as important, this experience expanded the Museum board's view of how they could do more to serve children and the community. Given the success in expanding their possibilities, they continued to search for additional creative, collaborative solutions.

Reflections

Which of your relationships are transactional versus relational?
Which relationships could be more valuable by transitioning
them to a more relational mode?
What would you have to do to become more relational?

FIND THE BEST FIT

—

Once you solidly operate from a relational mindset, one of the next imperatives in partnership building is being ruthless in finding the right fit. Partnerships are too much work to invest in without looking closely at fit. From the last section, DWB and Unilever were both fantastic organizations, but they weren't a good fit, and neither was water for CI. Unilever needed a nonprofit with supply chain capabilities. DWB couldn't offer that. Unilever did eventually find a perfect fit in Direct Relief. Direct Relief has excellent supply chain capabilities delivering medical supplies to thirty different countries for disaster relief activity.

You'll hear more about that later. Just remember that finding the right fit is worth the investment of time.

To hone the list of potential partners, some organizations start with identifying what is obviously off the table. The American Cancer Society (ACS) would never pair with a company that represented the opposite of its mission, to save lives from cancer. For example, since 30 percent of people who smoke will ultimately die from a smoking-related disease, and since lung cancer represents 22 percent of all cancer deaths, ACS would not partner with a tobacco company. After the obvious "no go" relationships are off the table, take plenty of time to find the perfect matches.

Even when you think you might have identified a perfect fit, continue to vet it. Be methodical to double-check what you think you know. One of the most outrageous examples I have of "knee jerk ill fit" was when Licopene, a powerful antioxidant found in tomatoes, was first correlated with cancer risk reduction. A well-known ketchup company was excited about this discovery and asked the American Cancer Society (ACS) to join them in an advertising campaign to be called "Until There Is a Cure, There's Ketchup." The company knew that the ACS name was well respected. The ACS voice behind this claim would surely boost sales. The company saw this as a natural fit. In their view, it even aligned with a key ACS criteria for partnerships: ingestibles had to be supported by science. Unfortunately, the fit was one-sided, and the science connection was poorly thought out.

Public trust is ACS's most powerful asset. Appearing to endorse something that is almost always eaten with food items that aren't good for cancer risk reduction (hot dogs, hamburgers, French fries) would not only erode public faith in ACS, it would betray it. The campaign never materialized. The company approached this conversation primarily from the perspective of their own gain. Had they completed more research beforehand, they would have discovered how damaging such a promotion would be for ACS's reputation and its goals for reducing cancer incidence.

"Look for common vision and mission and seek diversity of thought."

Ed Baker Professor, Georgia State University, and former Publisher of *Atlanta Business Chronicle*

Proper fit can be tricky. Here is an example. Science clearly supported an ACS connection with Campbell's Pork and Beans. The product is a healthy choice as long as you don't eat the accompanying lump of lard from the can. Personally, I don't know anyone who eats the lard. The problem wasn't science, it was perception. Unfortunately, at the time, our research indicated that the general public didn't perceive this product to be particularly healthy. We turned down this opportunity to partner because the effort and brand equity required to transform public opinion of the product was too high. The value exchange was lopsided. Those resources were better spent encouraging more consumption of foods the public already believed were healthy, but which they were not eating enough of, such as fresh fruits and vegetables.

ACS also turned down an opportunity to work with Coppertone. With skin cancer being the number one cancer in incidence, it might appear at first that this would be a good fit. There was one significant issue: positioning. Coppertone argued that you could tan safely, and their product would help you do that. ACS's position was that there was no such thing as a safe tan.

Keep in mind that not all issues carry the same taboo for similarly focused organizations. Susan G. Komen For The Cure is also a respected cancer-focused organization. Komen could align with certain topical or ingestible products that ACS simply could not. The essence of the ACS brand promise was to prevail over cancer through multiple activities, including research, patient support, and public advice on early detection and risk reduction. ACS is the trusted source for cancer information on par with physicians. People turn to ACS for opinions on cancer. Komen's brand promise was pure, simple, and powerful. They aim to fund the discovery of cures. The public didn't perceive Komen standing next to a less healthy food product as being an endorsement of that food. If ACS did, though, it could very well be perceived as having a connection to cancer risk reduction or a cure.

After eliminating the obvious no-go's, we have a list of potential partners. Many people would say that the next step is scheduling a meeting. If you've been in this business very long, you've heard people say that getting the right meeting with a prospective partner organization can take the most effort of all the steps involved in securing partnerships. Finding the right person who will see your offer as highly relevant is important, but that isn't where most of your time should be spent. If you don't dedicate at least half your time to making sure you are chasing the right partnership and then preparing for the uniqueness of that conversation, you might as well not show up. Proper selection and preparation should be 80 percent of the effort. This can be time-consuming and tedious, but it is essential.

This critical work starts with deeply understanding your own corporate or nonprofit organization's needs. The answer to need has to go deeper than money for the cause or looking like a good corporate citizen in front of a particular group of people. Some questions that can help you identify important needs are:

- What are the obstacles to your mission and vision?
- What situations plague your business model?
- What is the answer to the question of "if only we had . . ." we'd move mountains?
- What do your more successful competitors have that you don't?
- What capabilities and assets could boost your profit or nonprofit business?

The answers to these questions can help you build a list of requirements for prospects that have the potential for high relevance to your business. Additional screening will be necessary, and I suggest some criteria in the next section. But first, I can't overstate the importance of knowing what you need. You can then turn your attention to understanding what your potential partners need and how you are relevant to those needs. You may not be able to fit their strategies, criteria, or business needs, but if you do, you have a better chance of negotiating a partnership with them. Keep in mind that one partner's reason for being interested in you might be very different from others' reasons. It all comes down to relevance of the available value exchange.

A compelling fit with another entity can only come from finding out everything you can about them. Using formal research is very helpful, but be sure and look at news coverage and talk to people who know your prospects and their world well. The latter source can be the richest. As an example, through an acquaintance who worked for General Mills, I became educated on the complexities of the cereal category and pricing strategy struggles facing companies in this sector. Companies couldn't raise the price of a box of cereal by a penny without causing customer flight to other brands. I was interested in cereal because some brands met the American Cancer Society's science bar for healthy nutrition. ACS had no budget for nutrition advertising, so the right match with a cereal brand could pay for the dissemination of cancer risk reduction information. Research and experience told me that ACS could influence consumer consumption of healthy foods. In essence, ACS could help the right cereal brand with the pricing issue, and the company could help ACS disseminate an important public message. It worked really well. More on that later.

The point here is that this upfront wrestling with what you need and what your prospective partners need can reveal the core relevance behind a partnership. Those who don't start with a strong awareness of timely mutual needs will not identify optimal partners, nor will they be able to negotiate the most powerful agreements.

Reflections ⎯⎯⎯⎯⎯⎯⎯⎯⎯⎯⎯⎯⎯⎯⎯⎯

What partners have been your best fit? Why?

Which have been ill fit? Why?

What additional partner attributes would benefit you in the future?

How does this information shape your partner preferences going forward?

⎯⎯⎯⎯⎯⎯⎯⎯⎯⎯⎯⎯⎯⎯⎯⎯⎯⎯⎯⎯⎯⎯

TAILOR YOUR CRITERIA

Once you have created a list of prospective partners based on what you need and your relevancy to their needs, screen the list against additional selection criteria. Companies have been doing this for a long time to focus their support strategically in alignment with their business and foundation goals. Most companies today align their foundation strategies with their business objectives. One example of this is Coca-Cola's decade long 5x20 global initiative. The goal was to reach five million women in poverty with economic opportunity by 2020, and it was in alignment with Coke's supply chain objectives. This kind of "enlightened self-interest" is logical and is implemented with a win/win mindset. This purity of intent is the best pathway to doing well by doing good. Nonprofits who seek to help companies do well by doing good are likely to have greater partnership opportunities than those who hold an outdated notion that self-interest is a negative corporate character trait.

Corporate criteria for partnerships with nonprofits evolved for another very practical reason, too. While some companies may have deep pockets, none have enough money to say yes to all of the proposals that arrive at their doors. Strategic criteria provide a rationale for who can and who can't be considered for support. Articulating corporate criteria also saves time and resources for nonprofits by helping them discern upfront whether they are a good fit.

Similarly, nonprofits have strategies and needs which guide their targeting and selection of corporate partnership prospects. Nonprofits can't afford to waste their limited resources on partnerships that don't fit. At the American Cancer Society, we established ten criteria for corporate partnerships. I had board-level approval for my team to strike any deal with a corporation as long as it met the majority of these criteria. I reported to the board of directors on a quarterly basis about any new relationships to explain how each new agreement met our criteria. The criteria also helped align internal stakeholders and set the stage for being able to hold everyone accountable for deliverables committed in corporate agreements.

The ten point criteria created for the American Cancer Society were as follows:

1. Mission fit. The company could not be in conflict with the ACS mission. As previously noted, a relationship with a tobacco company would be the ultimate ill fit for ACS.

2. Alignment with brand positioning and issue statements. The Coppertone story from earlier is a good example of this. Coppertone wanted to partner on sunscreen related to reducing skin cancer, but ACS couldn't do it. Coppertone's position was that you could tan safely. ACS's position was that a safe tan isn't possible.

3. Proportional value. We had to know the tangible value of the relationship to the company, and ACS had to realize a fair and proportional value for the part we played. The relationship with Citi mentioned previously is a good example of achieving this.

4. Positive brand impact. Partnerships should create brand lift to both parties at the start but also throughout the life of the relationships. We added questions to the Gallup omnibus survey every other year to alert us to any negative public perceptions associated with our deals. ACS could not be used to "clean up" a corporate brand that was in trouble. All potential partners were researched to discover negative PR skeletons that could negatively impact ACS.

5. Low maintenance. We had limited resources and couldn't commit beyond what was reasonable for internal and local operations. Factors like PR support and any local ACS support for activation of partnerships had to be internally negotiated and agreed upon in advance.

6. Adherence to government regulations and guidelines. Our deals could not be structured in ways that might trigger unrelated business income tax or fly in the face of the construct of "truth in advertising."

7. Multi-year. The relationships were intended to be long-term so that all parties could fully realize the intended benefits.

8. No unlimited exclusivity and no direct endorsements. ACS knew its brand could influence buyer behavior and therefore felt that it was unethical to work exclusively with only one brand in a competitive space. For example, we were able to work with multiple brands in the tobacco cessation arena by limiting promotions with any one brand either by the time of the promotion so that it didn't overlap another promotion or by executing different promotions in different locations.

9. Low risk. No relationship comes without risk. Legal counsel would prefer no risk, but that isn't possible. We did have to articulate the rationale for deeming the relationship to be low risk.

10. Science backed. No partnerships around products that are ingestible or topical were allowed unless those products met scientific standards regarding cancer risk. For example, only seven of the twenty-eight cereal brands made by General Mills at the time we were negotiating met ACS's science standards.

These ACS criteria were tailor-fit to allow us to pursue any relationship that would further its mission while also protecting the organization from striking deals that could be risky. Every organization is different, and no one set of criteria can work for all. As previously mentioned, the Susan G. Komen Foundation for the Cure (Komen) is also a well-known, cancer-focused nonprofit, but they do not shy away from relationships with ingestible or topical products that might be considered unhealthy by scientific experts. This was not one of their criteria, nor should it have been. Komen didn't believe that their partnerships would drive the public opinion on the health of food or that they correlated with cancer risk reduction. They were right.

KFC was interested in Komen because it is a beloved organization and has a reputation as a very strong marketing partner. KFC wanted to increase their store traffic in order to increase sales. Engaging their customers and their employees in something that was meaningful to everyone was not only good for business, it was good for Komen, too.

KFC's promotion centered on giving 50 cents per bucket of fried chicken to Komen. To demonstrate that this was more than a simple promotion, KFC turned their chicken buckets pink for the promotion and listed all the names of their employees who had been impacted by breast cancer on pink ribbons inside KFC locations. Five thousand KFC franchisees collectively generated $4 million for Komen's breast cancer mission. The customers were happy, the employees were happy, and team Komen was happy. It was a beautiful partnership ingrained in the fabric of the company.

That said, not everyone was happy. Some professional nutritionists criticized Komen for linking its brand with a product that was deemed unhealthy for cancer patients. These naysayers felt the connection was a significant blunder because they felt it appeared to encourage people to eat fried chicken.

True to their reputation for standing their ground and inviting everyone to be an active part of the vision for a cure, Komen didn't put the chicken down. They celebrated this partnership for its open invitation allowing everyone to be a part of funding the cure. Other professionals offered additional reasons why the fit actually worked well. People with patient care backgrounds noted that when a person is sick with no appetite and losing weight at dangerous levels, offering food that tastes good and gives comfort is extremely helpful. Fundraisers were also quick to point out that the partnership raised a sizable amount of money, and they chanted, "No money, no mission."

"Hold tight to your criteria for the best strategic fit for partnerships and listen well."

Jo Ann Herold CEO, Herold Growth Consulting, former CMO Honeybaked Ham, former VP Brand Strategy Arby's, and Vice Chairman of Arby's Foundation

---

Finally, I want to emphasize that public perception is the final test of appropriate fit. The public didn't see the nutrition debate as relevant to the core value of this promotion. They saw this promotion as a way they could get involved and help find a cure for a dreaded disease that had touched their lives or someone close to them. This proposition was simple and compelling. The promotion resonated with KFC employees, customers and the public, it generated money for KFC and Komen, and it helped build awareness of screening to save lives.

I want to lean into my comment about standing your ground and gut instincts. Sometimes, as the KFC example shows, instincts are right on the mark. But occasionally, intuition can be off, so think a little more about it with me. A partnership or an element of a partnership can seem obvious. When an idea seems like a no-brainer, reluctance to spend research dollars to further prove it or massage it can feel wasteful. This unchecked confidence, however, can lead to sticky situations. I share the following story to suggest that research is always a good idea, whether or not something seems to be a no-brainer based on your criteria.

The Arthritis Foundation has participated in a number of successful corporate partnerships. They are good at it and have reached levels of respect and trust that support collaboration on new ideas. If one of their long-standing partners comes up with an interesting concept, they give it strong consideration. One particularly strong idea came from the Tide laundry detergent team. It was based on the knowledge that a strong consumer demographic of Tide product users was mature in age. Many in this older age group experienced joint stiffness, if not some level of motion-limiting arthritis. In an effort to resonate more with these consumers, Tide developed an easy-to-open package. They felt this was relevant and added value to their partner, the Arthritis Foundation. They invited Arthritis Foundation to join the launch of the new package design, which would also give the design more credibility in the eyes of buyers. The combination of the new package and an acknowledgement from the Arthritis Foundation was anticipated to lift sales.

The Arthritis Foundation thought this package innovation could benefit their community. They agreed to author a message to be printed on the box applauding Tide for helping people with arthritis. All should have been rosy. It seemed like a no-brainer.

Unfortunately, within a short time of the new package release, the Arthritis Foundation received calls from their community of patients and donors with a strange question. They wanted to know how the detergent should be applied to ease the pain of arthritis. No one anticipated that customers might assume detergent could be used topically to ease pain. They were shocked. I honestly don't know if this public misunderstanding could have been caught with some advance research. That said, research can often catch such problems, and problems are much less expensive to address before a package, product, or campaign launch than afterward.

Now that we've made a convincing case for tight criteria and research related to finding the right partnership fit, let's talk about when to break with your criteria. You may find this counterintuitive, but knowing when to make exceptions to your criteria is very important.

At ACS, no partnership could hit all of our criteria. We had to make judgment calls, just like any company does. A good corporate example comes from AT&T, which at the time was the nation's second largest single brand advertised with a budget of $2 billion. AT&T used strong criteria for partnerships, which helped them fend off the barrage of solicitations from worthy causes. Be sure to have a rationale for saying no because no matter how much money you have, you don't have enough to fund everything. AT&T's criteria at that time focused on one key objective: education. Specifically, the company focused on college-level math and engineering since it related directly to their current and future workforce needs.

Sometimes AT&T would ignore this strategic focus on education. Why in the world would any company spend so much time developing criteria if it wasn't always going to use the criteria all the time? This usually happens when there were other, unique considerations at play. Sometimes, those unique things were political forces. For example, to be a good corporate citizen in the eyes of those who ran the city of Atlanta, AT&T would need to invest in some things that weren't perfectly aligned with the company's strategy. The investments were aligned with the bigger picture needs of the city in which they did business. Another AT&T objective was to be seen as a good corporate citizen in the eyes of city leadership and customers. Savvy nonprofits that didn't fit AT&T's core criteria might still be a fit via their relevance to the City of Atlanta's goals and ambitions.

This brings to mind the phrase "strange bedfellows," which occurs when parties that are normally unlikely to agree find a powerful reason to work together. I mention this because there are all kinds of situations, market disruptions, or unanticipated opportunities that can justify relaxing or shifting your partnership fit criteria. Keep an eye on trends and events that impact your business objectives. Sifting such information can reveal new needs and partner prospects.

The COVID-19 pandemic brought unlikely partnerships. As many businesses and service models faltered, some corporate and nonprofit organizations came together to cope better together than alone. Children International was seriously impacted during COVID, but they pivoted to keep their mission of empowering children to lift themselves out of poverty alive. CI normally works by placing safe centers in dense urban slums. In these locations, kids can see doctors and dentists, use computers, get help with schoolwork, and build their confidence. All that good work was in jeopardy when COVID forced them to close their facilities.

In Honduras, CI chose to focus on two new urgent needs for the kids: a lack of food and waning hope. CI repurposed money they had been using to run the centers to buy food. Unfortunately, they didn't have a way to deliver it, so they needed a partner. The local government in Honduras had trucks, but another major hurdle existed. Staff would encounter significant risk by driving and unloading valuable cargo in areas with a heavy gang presence. They needed another partner. The one entity the gangs respected and would not harm was the Catholic church. These circumstances birthed the unlikely and beautiful partnership between the local Honduran government, CI, and the church. Families not only received food, but they felt hope as well. Moreover, each partner witnessed greater local respect and appreciation.

Reflections

How do your partner criteria reflect your business needs?

How do your criteria reduce risk?

How does your criteria sharpen your ability to speed up the identification of best matches for your needs?

When have you (or would you) break your criteria?

LEARN TO NEGOTIATE

This business basic might seem a bit too basic for some. Negotiation can seem easy, especially if all the homework regarding relevant alignment and the value of assets has been completed.

One might think that conversation about the details of value exchange and working together would now flow naturally. If that were really the case, we wouldn't see so many great courses on negotiating. Beyond the academics of it, negotiation takes practice. It is as much art as science, and a whole different kettle of fish from soliciting a gift.

In nonprofits, the responsibility for researching and building partnerships with corporations is often given to major donor fundraising teams because there are similarities between the art of securing gifts of significant size and building robust partnerships. In terms of similarities, major donor operations are relational by nature. It takes time to understand a donor's motivation and passion and match that with a proposal that fits. Large donor investments are also highly correlated to long-term relationships founded on mutual respect and nurtured by good stewardship. Additionally, the best donor engagement efforts generate not just money, but a strong desire to advocate for the cause and encourage others to participate with their time, talents and treasure. The similarity doesn't stop there. Like companies, these large donors often see themselves as investors and conversations with them can involve enlightened self-interest. Their motivations can range from a genuine desire to impact a social condition to creating a legacy or modeling behavior for their children and grandchildren. Wealthy individuals might also be motivated to please friends, cement connections with other influential people, or live out their faith.

In fact, all of the factors mentioned above are at play with corporate partnership engagement. The difference is that partnerships are rooted in business value exchanges. This focus creates a host of extra complexities that major gift officers may not be experienced in handling.

The necessity of "speaking the same language" when negotiating is a good example of the different nature of corporate engagement. Speaking the same language is important in donor relations, but there are differences. In donor relations, if the donor is deeply faith-based, things will go better if the account representative can relate to and reference similar faith language. For example, I once had a lovely donor who believed deeply in guidance from the deceased (people and animals) and the power of crystals. Fortunately, I had a team member who was genuinely curious about the unknown and held no judgment of others' beliefs and curiosities. She was able to communicate genuinely with the donor, and they connected beautifully. Another donor we had was essentially a happy hippy and very artsy. My team member who was responsible for that region was "all Wall Streety" and, for the life of him, could not flex his persona. He used a whole different language in word and dress and attitude. We had to reassign that account. These personalities and many more can all be present in the boardroom as well as in the living room, but the dominant language in partnerships is going to be business. The conversation in the boardroom will be distinctly different from the conversation in the living room. Those responsible for corporate engagement will be more successful if they are fluent in business speak.

So exactly how does business language and perspective create different dynamics in negotiation of partnerships? Foremost is the knowledge of business itself. Business gain and ROI need to be topics of discussion. Some fundraisers can't easily incorporate these kinds of business topics which handicaps them. Additionally, if a fundraiser displays some subtle (or not-so-subtle) negative judgment about the necessity for a company to have a return on investment, this can cause negotiations to falter. Individuals holding critical judgments of their potential partners don't usually excel in negotiations. Even if the lead contact for the nonprofit "gets it" with regard to the business orientation of negotiations, things can still veer off course if others on the nonprofit team simply don't "get it." For example, nonprofit program experts are often fully immersed in mission with that program work being their primary language. They can have trouble jibing with people who are not fundamentally motivated as they are.

A good example of partners who successfully negotiated a powerful relationship while navigating complicated issues involves The Coca-Cola Company and World Wildlife Foundation. The leaders of these two great organizations asked their respective staffs to explore how they might work together strategically around water use and conservation. The initial staff reaction in both organizations was less than enthusiastic. Some people just couldn't see how a company with a problematic reputation for its use of water sources could authentically pair with an organization that was all about conservation and ethical use of water. Finding common ground took work and patience. Thankfully, they did put in the work and created one of the most successful partnerships in the world.

Success for this partnership is credited to the commitment they had for transparent communications about each others' capabilities, needs, and challenges. This yielded the trust and information needed to negotiate a relationship that neither anticipated could be so powerful. Both sides not only understood each other better, they developed deep appreciation for each other's commitment to improving the world and the integrity with which they approached their respective business goals. In fact, their goals aligned quite well. Together, they created an inspiring, best practice model for blending business needs with significant impact on protecting water sources.

Water4 is another great example of the power of thoughtful negotiations underpinned by deep knowledge of context and partner circumstances. What is additionally interesting about this example is that it goes beyond a profit entity working with nonprofits and local governments. It includes local people who stand to benefit from solving the problem of access to water. Water4 drills and revitalizes water wells. Loans are provided to pay for this work and make it possible for people to create water-centered businesses. In this model, local people are no longer relegated to the sole position of beneficiary. An economy is created around clean water. Local people can engage as entrepreneurs. They not only take part in the creation of wells, they create water-based businesses. This is the foundation for an economy that solves problems beyond the availability of water. It ultimately powers solutions to complex problems that have jeopardized the lives and livelihoods of millions around the world. Water plus jobs enables the improvement of schools and health systems.

Water4 partners start with a common business vision for bringing a permanent water supply solution. This vision disrupts traditional approaches that give water away without making sure that the water and water systems remain viable over time. It makes sure local communities have the money to fix wells when they break and buy parts when needed. In this negotiation, minds shift, creating a belief in possibilities versus pity. People begin to operate from a mental perspective of abundance rather than scarcity. This positions them as powerful, not helpless. The impact of this approach is amazing. Water4 has helped create a permanent water supply for two million people, with 650 local business partners and 4000 utility points.

The ability to negotiate is a skill and part of a business mindset. The job is to build a case for an exchange in value. To do this, be definite about what you have that is of value to your prospective partner, and make sure you know what the asset is worth to them. You can't negotiate a fair deal if you don't know this. Be willing to walk away if you can't get what is fair. This, then, is the key difference between negotiating a deal and asking for a donation.

Reflections

For nonprofits, does your lead partnership staff have experience in business negotiations? Have they ever walked away from a deal because they couldn't reach a fair exchange of value? If you haven't ever walked away, you likely are asking more than negotiating

For companies, does your lead partnership staff have experience in nonprofit business matters? Do they take the time to know the needs of the nonprofit partner? Do they really know what assets they have and their value to the nonprofit?

Have you ever felt you weren't speaking the same language as your prospective partner? How could bridging the language gap have helped?

PUT EVERYTHING IN WRITING

—

This may sound harsh: If it isn't in writing, it isn't real. Yes, you may find examples of relationships working well on a handshake. I would like the world to work that way all the time, but it doesn't. I did my undergraduate work in Japan, where honoring your word is a strong cultural value. I remember feeling disillusioned after reading that Japanese companies shifted to written contracts because oral agreements were painfully inadequate when negotiating with Western companies.

Partnerships between companies and nonprofits also function best with contracts and written agreements. Without these, we are at the mercy of individual memory of details related to negotiations. Memory and intent can change if the viability of an agreement wanes. This can happen when people leave positions, when markets change, or when costs exceed expectations. Especially in volatile and dynamic economic times, maintaining agreements in writing as a foundation for renegotiation is best.

Having written agreements becomes even more important as the complexity of a partnership grows. Clear documentation of what each party will deliver is essential, along with identifying the resources to be committed when the parties start working together. Specificity is important. Do you want increased sales, shifts in public opinion, or alleviation of a social condition? Everyone needs to agree on the goals so they can measure results and know if the partnership is successful. Actions need to be documented and accountability measured.

A good contract takes the mystery out of what short and long-term success looks like. For example, when the American Cancer Society partnered with the Florida Department of Citrus, both entities had specific outcomes in mind. ACS wanted the public to learn about healthy nutrition and to choose healthy foods while the FDOC wanted to sell more juice. At the time of this partnership, juice consumption had taken a dive. Many people attributed this trend to excellent marketing of cola products. The Coca-Cola Company had successfully gained dominance in what they referred to as "share of stomach." Cola was fast becoming the drink of choice, period. The ACS/FDOC contract specified how their respective objectives would be measured and ultimately created a tangible scorecard to celebrate. FDOC measured sales and public recall of the health message from advertising. We succeeded on both fronts.

Let's pause a minute and talk about how this success came to happen. It isn't enough just to be of one mind on the ultimate goals for the partnership. Working together to get there is important. For example, an important factor that the partners needed to honor was each other's opinions and feelings on message strategy. FDOC wanted to use humor in television ads. Humor wasn't really an approach used by ACS. Suspending our concerns about the combination of humor and cancer took some effort. I'm glad we did.

Close your eyes and envision this ad. A mom is driving her

car with nice music playing. The back seat has grocery bags packed next to her young son's car seat. Suddenly, the radio announcer breaks in to say, "This just in from the American Cancer Society. Juice as part of a healthy diet can reduce your chance of cancer." The child's eyes grow wide, and he grabs a jug of juice from the bag next to him and begins gulping it down. He then throws the empty jug out the window and wipes his mouth with a huge grin. The ad was memorable and made people smile. We took flack from people who cared about littering, but, all in all, the campaign moved the needle on awareness of healthy nutrition and sold juice.

Now, back to the exciting topic of contracts. From a nonprofit perspective, standing up for what you want in a contract might feel a little like the David and Goliath story. Nobody wanted to go up against Goliath because he was so big and powerful. The Israelites certainly didn't think it was possible to set fair rules of fight. Nonprofits sometimes think companies hold all the cards and that they don't have the power to negotiate for what they need. That isn't true if the partnership holds significant value for the company. Be bold. Ask for what you need. Negotiate for what is fair.

Here is an example of asking for what you need. At the ACS, I didn't have a large budget for measuring market behavior. If I was going to convince a big company that partnering with ACS could mean an uptick in sales, I had to have market data to prove it. Evidence of ROI is power in negotiating and maintaining partner agreements. To deal with my lack of money, I spent other people's money. Especially after I had the FDOC story, I could ask a prospective corporate partner to conduct the necessary test research to prove impact on their business. The research design for proof of test and ongoing tracking was defined and included in contracts. Sometimes tracking research or impact research didn't cost the company anything either. They sometimes just added a question or two to a study the company already had planned to do or an extra query of data they had already collected. Some figures, especially sales data, were especially sensitive and proprietary. We found two ways of increasing comfort with access to sales data. One was to focus on measuring a bump in sales over a period of time rather than actual sales. However, with proper non-disclosure agreements, companies might share specific sales data too, especially when the data is important to measure progress toward a key goal of the partnership.

Our work with the Florida Department of Citrus (FDOC) involved them adding questions about consumer perception of juice as a healthy product to their research and sharing data related to change in juice sales. Had we not agreed in writing to sharing data like this, someone could have changed their mind about it. In that case, we wouldn't have been able to concretely demonstrate the partnership's value or impact. We would be weaker in ongoing negotiations without this information. ACS needed to know if the ad created through the partnership developed new consumer knowledge of healthy nutrition, and the FDOC needed to know if sales grew. To continue to build on what we started, we both needed to know what kind of progress we both were making. Knowing this, we could talk about the fair, proportional value of the relationship.

I think we were blessed to have great results right away with the FDOC relationship. More often, desired results like we saw with FDOC take time. For this reason, partner agreements with audacious goals—like impacting perceptions and sales—should be multi-year. The longer timeline allows partners to establish baselines and evaluate change over time. The evaluation prompts natural modifications of partner efforts. This collaborative testing and tweaking can lead to greater success.

Another important aspect of written agreements is that they should be short—just long enough to cover the essentials. Put all the other "boilerplate" legal protections in an addendum. If you don't, you'll have 25-page legal agreements. Long legal documents are scary. They also take too much time to review and pass muster with each party's legal staff. I've seen legal reviews take months. As time goes by, circumstances can change. You can lose a relationship before it has a chance to launch if its relevance fades with changing circumstances as you wait for legal reviews. Luckily, at ACS we had a fantastic head of the legal department. He treated my team as an internal customer with unique needs rather than a rogue group that needed to be corralled. He understood that we could never reduce risk to zero and that trying to do so through a contract could drastically limit our ability to close deals. We found common ground on a reasonable tolerance for risk, and our board approved criteria for partnerships. Together, we were able to create a two-page template for corporate cause marketing agreements infused with both business and legal perspectives. The business language was up front, and all the standard legalese on protections found its way into an addendum.

One last note on contracts. With testing and results in hand and agreements in writing, you really have to deliver. At World Vision, some of our corporate grant partners would fund specific projects, like drilling wells for safe water. This money often had to be used in a given timeframe so that the companies could see results. Deadlines prevent nonprofits from sitting on the money for an extended period. If a nonprofit fails to use the money on time, the contract allows the company to request the money back. Contingencies can't always be anticipated when working in developing countries. I've found companies to be quite understanding as long as they are well informed and never surprised. That said, because various organizations have repeatedly struggled to fulfill their commitments, corporations and their foundations have developed more rigorous contractual requirements for deliverables. The big takeaway: don't agree to it if you can't do it.

Reflections

When in your experience would it have been helpful to have had agreements in writing? What specific elements do you wish you had in a contract?

How has specificity in a contract helped you manage a relationship better?

What difficulties have you experienced that were caused by partners inability to hold each other accountable?

TEST IT, PROVE IT

—

I don't know of many big partnerships that didn't include a test to either prove a concept or to make sure that partners could deliver on promises. As we saw in the previous section, this kind of testing can help you understand value which is key to negotiating contracts. Beyond that, testing can also create a sense of common vested interest. When data resolves concerns about working together, people feel more confident of success and more willing to invest resources. If a test fails to resolve problems or shine a light on how to mitigate concerns, the partnership likely never sees rollout. Nor should it. Abandoning a weak idea saves everyone time and money. Hopefully, everyone works in a place that believes in "failing forward"—always learning and never being punished for experiments that fail to meet expectations. I believe we learn from what works, but sometimes we learn even more from what doesn't work. At any rate, this process builds trust and respect while providing hard data upon which you can continue to build.

Proceeding without testing may not be risky for some simple agreements, but forgoing research can sink complex relational partnerships. Investment in research should match the degree of complexity. Combined with transparent conversation around test results, data enables relationships to pivot and weather predicted and unforeseen challenges. This promotes a collaborative spirit while generating more comfort with risk as issues are identified. In this dynamic, parties don't blame each other when pilots don't go as planned. Failure is seen as a part of the puzzle of eventual and even greater success. Working jointly and fluidly while growing what's known builds a strong team with pride in the collective discovery of solutions.

Let's dig in here. If a nonprofit identifies how their capabilities can address a significant problem for a company, they are on the road to creating a powerful partnership. Their job, however, isn't to solve companies' problems, just like companies don't sit around looking for ways to solve nonprofit business issues. Doing so only makes sense when such an effort has a significant impact on your own business, too. Feeding America's rocketing success from a $20 million nonprofit to over a billion a year is such a story.

Feeding America believed they could solve a problem facing companies selling perishable foods. The solution also offered significant benefit to their mission of feeding the poor. The companies' reality was that a percentage of the perishable food in their stores would spoil before they could sell it. The unsold food went to the dump. They lost significant amounts of money on wasted food and on employee time spent handling the disposal. Feeding America offered to pick up and deliver food to local food banks before its expiration date. Sam's Clubs was interested, but they needed proof that Feeding America could in fact deliver. (Pun intended.) They feared bad press if expired food ended up being distributed to those in need.

The test worked! When Feeding America continued to deliver without issue, the success caught the eye of Walmart and others who were experiencing the same food waste problem. The idea grew, resulting in a tremendous number of food insecure people being fed, a powerful win for all.

The impact for the companies was bigger than the money saved on food disposal. It was bigger than the saved employee time. The companies secured tax credits for the donation of food. Customers and employees also loved the idea, so they earned a halo to boot. A huge loss was turned into an advantage for all because a nonprofit had a bold idea that they could execute well.

Not all testing stories turn out like the Feeding America and Sam's Club story. Sometimes, we think we can do something and, try as we may, we can't. Refrain from testing something you aren't pretty darn sure you can do. When I was at Children International, the Walmart Family Foundation expressed interest in replicating CI programs being delivered in Title I schools around Little Rock, Arkansas. CI, on the other hand, wanted to grow the program where they had the experience, support, and staffing in place. Replication in a new area would take more than money. Every community is unique and requires time to build local support for new interventions.

CI was excited about the prospect of working with the foundation to expand its services to children in need. If the partnership worked, it would be a long-term relationship that could dramatically impact educational attainment for children from impoverished backgrounds. That said, the new area was very different from Little Rock. Our program wasn't cookie-cutter in nature. We depended on local relationships where mutual respect and trust had been built over time. CI was smart to listen to their local program staff who didn't believe they could expand into a new area on the timeline expected during the pandemic. The effort would be costly, and the drain on staff could negatively impact existing work in the Little Rock area.

In the end, CI decided to decline the partnership and likely buoyed its reputation by being transparent about the rationale. Not many nonprofits turn down money. It was courageous to do so, and the action earned us a good degree of respect.

Not to talk out of both sides of my mouth about testing, but sometimes you don't have time. A time-sensitive opportunity may present itself, forcing you to go with the best information available. The advantages are so great, or the implications of not acting are so dire that you must move without testing. In the last example, CI felt no urgency to act and felt significant apprehension about trying. The story previously told about Children International's Honduras staff reaching out to the local municipality and the local Catholic church to provide food during the pandemic is a good example of urgency driving speed. They didn't have time to test. People were starving. The idea seemed sound to all, and, thankfully, the plan worked.

When you must move quickly, be sure to communicate well with all stakeholders. This allows you to tap everyone's knowledge, creativity, and gut instincts. Good paths forward can emerge from this, but sometimes emotions can interfere. Emotions are just as unpredictable as other disruptors and often happen at inopportune times, creating short windows for resolution.

Now, let's look at a story involving the Special Olympics Austria Games and Microsoft, where partnership leaders found a quick and creative fix to a problem that could have destroyed the relationship. They certainly had no time to test options. Leading up to the 2017 games, the International Special Olympics (SO) secured Microsoft's support for $10.6 million. This figure included hard costs of promotions and hardware/platform donations. The deal was celebrated at SO headquarters but not initially received well locally. Headquarters had made the agreement without consent from the local oversight committee for sponsorships. Global staff couldn't wait for the formation of the local committee to pursue the deal. Unfortunately, this rationale and a heartfelt apology weren't enough to resolve the internal problem. Local staff and volunteers didn't appreciate being left out of a process they were charged with leading. This became more than an uncomfortable internal squabble when the local group left Microsoft out of a major display at the games. Sponsors who had been part of the local process had their logos displayed prominently on the ice rink. There was no time to explore other ways to give equal visibility to Microsoft or to prove their value. After some quick thinking, SO saved the day by placing Microsoft banners around the rink. This actually provided greater visibility than the painted logos on the ice and positioned Microsoft well as the event's largest sponsor.

Reflections

When have you tested a concept before rolling it out? How did that impact the relationship and the structure of the deal?

What other relationships do you have that could benefit from piloting an idea?

When did you "go with your gut" with a good outcome? What factors helped you make the decision to trust your gut? What lessons did you learn from the experience?

ELEVATE ROI

—

Whether you represent the corporate or nonprofit side of the equation in a partnership, you must realize a return on your investment (ROI). The agreement has to be worth the time, resources, and money put into it. With insufficient benefit, the relationship will falter if it ever launches in the first place. Let's highlight this with a story from Kurt Aschermann, retired CMO for the Boys and Girls Clubs of America (BGCA). He shared it with me years ago, and it still resonates. He emphasizes how nonprofits need to be keenly aware of corporations' business objectives and the tangible goals that define success in their eyes.

Kurt led many partner relationships for BGCA and was respected throughout the sector for his work with corporations. He had great people skills, and he focused on partners who shared a passion for the BGCA mission of lifting kids out of poverty. One day, he learned a lesson that he never forgot.

This story begins with Kurt recalling how confidently he walked into a large bank's conference room to review highlights of what he felt had been an extremely successful relationship. With enthusiasm, he presented various indicators, including the number of media impressions generated, the number of bank volunteers involved, and the number of underprivileged children who received assistance. He loved meetings like this.

As he shared the good news, Kurt's corporate counterpart sat quietly, holding two pieces of paper. Upon finishing the presentation, Kurt's pride shifted to concern when he noted the unimpressed look on his partner's face. Such uncomfortable moments of silence can seem so very long. Finally, the banker slowly slid the papers across the table to Kurt. Identical graphs, except for the dates, spoke a thousand words. One graph showed credit card usage before the beginning of the partnership. The other chart showed credit use at the conclusion of the promotion. No change. The graphs revealed no growth, which was the key motivation for the bank's investment in sponsoring BGCA promotions. In this moment, regardless of all the positive news and good feelings, Kurt saw that the partnership had missed the mark. Unless BGCA could pivot to address the bank's key success indicator, growth in credit card usage, the future of the relationship was certainly not assured. Good works done well and the positive feelings that come from them are not enough to keep large investors investing.

In fact, being relevant to a partner's primary concerns can be the deciding factor on whether you can even initiate a partnership discussion. This was the situation between the American Cancer Society and General Mills. We believed that partnering could lift cereal sales while increasing the public's knowledge of healthy foods. The challenge was convincing General Mills that public association of their healthy products with a deadly disease would be good for business.

Cereal manufacturers weren't apt to take even small chances with messaging given the significant sensitivity to pricing within the category. An acquaintance working at General Mills told me that a one penny increase on a box of cereal was enough to send loyal customers scurrying to other competitive brands of cereal. I had to provide impressive proof that associating with ACS was not only safe for their image, but that it would make more money for them.

"Listen to what your partner is trying to do or solve and create real ROI together."

Kirsten Suto Seckler Chief Marketing and Communications Officer, Shatterproof, and former Chief Brand and Marketing Officer for Special Olympics

---

To prove impact in terms of ROI, we conducted quantitative market research in four U.S. markets. We identified high traffic locations where we were likely to intercept people meeting the profile of healthy cereal consumers. We showed these health-conscious cereal consumers a mock advertisement. The ad informed them that, according to ACS, the healthy cereal shown was part of a diet that can reduce the risk of cancer. The copy also said that a percentage of the sale of the cereal would go to help find cures for cancer. Finally, we asked the people reading this ad how much more, if any, they would likely pay for a box of this cereal if a portion of the sale went to the American Cancer Society.

Our findings were compelling. On average, research participants said they would pay 25 cents more for a box of cereal if a portion went to ACS. Of course, some people would pay absolutely nothing more while others would pay significantly more than a quarter. Even if respondents inflated their enthusiasm for higher pricing, the findings demonstrated a tolerance for increase dramatically more than the penny General Mills thought was the top threshold. We had quantitative data showing that ACS could dramatically impact pricing in the cereal category. Additionally, we knew people would think more highly of cereal associated with the beloved ACS brand.

Through a friend, I was able to get a fifteen-minute meeting with a brand manager at General Mills. Knowing that the window would be short, I decided to bring one piece of paper to the meeting, a bell curve showing the 25 cents average increase that consumers said they would pay for cereal associated with ACS. When I arrived, I could tell that the brand manager was indeed very busy and not terribly excited about fitting me into his schedule. I thanked him for his time and placed the bell curve in front of him. Our fifteen minutes turned into an hour-long conversation that ultimately generated $1.5 million for ACS over three years. ROI is king.

The ROI for both parties in the ACS/General Mills partnership was strong. In addition to money from the license agreement, ACS realized millions of dollars of value for nutrition education because the health message was disseminated in General Mills' ads and on their cereal boxes. ACS couldn't afford advertising dollars for nutrition messaging and was able to ride General Mills advertising to accomplish this. Such deals helped move the needle on consumer awareness of the benefit of healthy nutrition choices. The partnership was also valuable to General Mills both from a sales and product positioning perspective.

Reflections ————————————————————————

Do you know the tangible gains you and your partner expect to realize?

Do you have any relationships that have weak ROI for either party? If so, how can you improve ROI?

What might be the overarching gain for your organization if you calculated a tangible ROI for all your partnerships?

COMPLY WITH REGULATIONS

—

Regulation sometimes seems burdensome to me. I understand that it saves lives to wear seat belts and drive at safe speeds. I'm convinced that universal background checks for guns would help keep citizens safe, too. And I do prefer a world with limits on how much the wealthy can spend to influence elections. So even though I might not like some regulations, I firmly believe that regulation within reason is good and can prevent the abuse of power. Until we live in a world where everyone demonstrates absolute integrity and good judgment all the time, we need some regulation. Thinking like this made me feel better about the eighteen months that the IRS spent combing my books at ACS looking for violations on nonprofit relationships with companies.

The IRS had become interested in nonprofits' corporate engagement activities after hearing about some of the more successful partnerships between companies and nonprofits at the time. They saw a potential case for unrelated business income tax (UBIT) on nonprofits in some situations. Specifically, they felt that the ACS partnership with the Florida Department of Citrus might be one of those situations. If the IRS decided that ACS was directly selling juice, that would fall outside our mission. Gain on non-mission activity can trigger tax on that gain.

The success of the FDOC and ACS partnership was also noticed by other important oversight groups, including the Attorneys General offices in New York and Florida. They were not so concerned about tax as they were about nonprofits appearing to endorse specific company products, like aspirin for arthritis or juice for health. They believed that such direct or indirect endorsements swayed public behavior and could be used to build corporate profits thereby taking perhaps inappropriate advantage of charitable missions. They were concerned that a nonprofit might unwittingly allow use of their names and logos in a manner that could misguide consumers. In essence, the Attorneys General offices wanted to make sure that there was "truth in advertising" related to any direct or implied endorsements.

In essence, government entities were and still are sensitive to corporate and nonprofit partnerships. They want any nonprofit involvement resulting in greater sales for companies' products to be above reproach. That said, even relationships that are executed ethically can trigger unrelated business income tax (UBIT) for the nonprofit. Sometimes, it might be well worth it to pay the tax. However, it is wise to be well versed in the rules for partnerships because if ethical lapses are discovered, all partners could be in legal jeopardy and could face fines.

ACS came out of all the scrutiny smelling like a rose. The attorneys general spent a few hours meeting with me and ACS's chief financial officer to discuss their concerns. We sincerely appreciated their guidance on the finer points of truth in advertising and appropriate relationships between nonprofits and companies. The conversation helped us refine our criteria and the guardrails for our partnerships. The IRS conversations were more challenging. They spent months making sure our corporate alliances were designed appropriately. ACS was fortunate to have excellent internal finance and legal partners that had structured passive agreements with companies. ACS was not actively selling juice or cereal, and we had control over any messaging that used our name. Yes, the ACS was present in grocery stores, handing out nutrition information and answering nutrition questions. We were standing by the folks selling juice, but we didn't sell juice.

The experience with oversight groups also impressed upon me how important it was to be absolutely clear in the consumer-facing language used in cause marketing. Clarity of the offer and language is in the best interest of companies, nonprofits, and the consumer. Our relationships with FDOC and General Mills honored this litmus test. That said, government review doesn't always turn out wonderfully for everyone. More than half of the states in the U.S. have commercial co-venture laws that impact cause marketing promotions. These laws regulate marketing practices involving charitable campaigns to consumers. Each state enforces their statutes with fines. For severe infractions, states can enforce criminal consequences. In 1999, Yoplait ran a promotion benefitting the Breast Cancer Research Foundation with a capped donation, but they didn't reveal the cap. They simply promised consumers that the company would donate 50 cents a lid. Customers weren't aware of the limit on the donation until they bought the product and lifted the lid off. After this was drawn to their attention, Yoplait's parent company General Mills made amends by making an additional $63,000 donation to cover the total lid collection efforts of Georgia customers.

Be sure you understand the regulations in place about partnerships between profit and nonprofit organizations. Most certainly abide by them. To falter on this point can be costly in terms of fines, but also in terms of reputation.

Reflections

Have you run partnership promotions without a sufficient legal review of its customer promises?

Are there any partnerships wherein the nonprofit is actively selling a product or service? If so, is the nonprofit willing to pay UBIT on those gains?

OPERATE ETHICALLY

—

This might sound a bit trite, but bear with me. Ethics is an appropriate point upon which to close this chapter on business basics. We all know individuals who may sacrifice a bit of purity of soul to achieve a greater good or sometimes for personal gain. Personal gain can take different shapes. Sometimes the gain is money, but it can be status or simply protecting one's job. Stepping into a gray area on ethics for any reason usually comes with a narrative and rationale as to why it was necessary to do so. In my opinion, ill gotten gain is tainted no matter how good the excuse is. Such action will come back to haunt you.

Here are some ethical considerations to keep in mind:

Be pure in motive when partnering. Nonprofit brands should never be used to superficially position a company as good in the face of bad deeds. Nor should they be used to clean up a public relations issue for a company.

Achieve a fair balance of value given for value received. Companies shouldn't lowball nonprofits for use of their assets, and nonprofits must negotiate with knowledge of what their assets are worth. Citibank showed ethical grounding when they agreed to use data to determine the financial gain to them from use of the ACS name on their credit card. As described earlier, data drove that deal from an initial offer of $150,000 a year to $15 million over five years.

Be accountable. Document your promises contractually. Don't exaggerate what you can deliver. Do what you commit to do in the time frame promised.

Trust and verify. Be transparent. Let data tell the story. Partnerships based on tangible outcomes will last much longer than those built on feelings.

Be reasonable and fact-based. Both in negotiations and evaluations.

Keep what is best for consumers and beneficiaries in mind. Do no harm. Partnerships that don't have the best interests of the public or beneficiaries as a primary objective should never see the light of day.

Co-create, co-evaluate, co-pivot. You are in a partnership. No unilateral decisions.

Part ways with respect. Whether the partnership was a success or a failure or somewhere in between, always take the high road as you disengage. Part ways with respect and honor.

This seems like a good place to talk about the "Think Before You Pink" campaign launched by the nonprofit watchdog organization, Breast Cancer Action (BCA) in 2002. The program is still running strong today because BCA feels that some companies aren't holding themselves to a high bar with regard to ethics and fairness.

BCA is a group of breast cancer activists alarmed by what they felt was a shallow promotional focus on pink ribbons and disease awareness generating an inordinate amount of money for companies with a paltry amount of money generated for the broader cause. Sometimes, companies "went pink" as a way of solving other public relations issues that were weakening the company brand in some way. To right this perceived injustice, part of what BCA does is to expose the companies whom they feel "pink wash" themselves as powerful advocates of the breast cancer cause when in fact they do little for the cause. One example is BCA's 2021 Think Before You Pink campaign called "Stop Banking on Breast Cancer," which called out the partnership between Susan G. Komen Foundation and

Bank of America. The Susan G. Komen Pink Ribbon Banking Program generated funds for their cause from credit and debit card use. BCA saw this campaign as ill use of the goodwill of the breast cancer community because it increased profit for Bank of America, which provided financing for the fossil fuel industry, which is linked to cancer.

The moral of the story is to hold yourself to a high bar on ethics. You can't make everyone happy, and you may endure criticism anyway, but making sure you engage, continue, and end partnerships with the highest ethical standards will serve everyone well.

Reflections

What examples have you seen of partners operating in the gray area of ethics? What was the price paid for this in terms of fines and reputation?

What does operating in the gray area of ethics do to trust?

Chapter 2

INVENTORY ASSETS & CREATE FAIR VALUE EXCHANGE

The last chapter dealt with some select business basics. You can't build partnerships well without knowing how to operate from a business perspective. This chapter delves into three issues that are more complicated. First, to make powerful partnerships, companies and nonprofits must know what assets they have and what they are worth to potential partners. Nonprofits do not have a great reputation for recognizing their assets from a company's perspective. Companies can also fail to recognize what they have that might be of interest to nonprofits beyond money. Once you recognize that you may have an interesting asset to a potential partner, you can then determine the asset's worth. Finally, you must negotiate a fair exchange of value. Parties should ensure proportionate value throughout the partnership.

ASSESS ASSETS FROM
AN INVESTOR PERSPECTIVE

—

If you ask most companies and nonprofits to list their assets, they'll usually focus first on bricks and mortar and other tangibles; however, the intangibles can actually be more valuable than the tangible. Interbrand, a global brand valuation company, once stated that The Coca-Cola company's name was more valuable than all of its physical structures. In some situations, some brands like the American Cancer Society examples I've shared, can move consumer behavior, which can be quite valuable. Anything endorsed by Oprah can go from obscurity to fame rather quickly. Other examples of intangibles include intellectual property, staff expertise, or human networks.

Knowing what your assets are from your own business perspective is important, but when you deal in partnerships, you must understand them from the lens of potential partners. Failure to do this may result in over- or undervaluing them. For example, non-functioning water wells in Africa were seen as useless until Water4 refurbished them and turned them into sustainable assets. Accurately valuing all your assets gives you the information necessary to negotiate beautiful relationships. Value can vary for different potential partners and in different situations. Direct Relief has a fantastic supply chain operation. This is valuable to someone who doesn't have that superpower and needs it. If your partner doesn't need to move a product globally, that capability isn't worth anything to them. You have to look at your assets through the eyes of a potential partner to have the strongest negotiating position.

Let's now look at the relationship between the American Cancer Society (ACS) and Citibank, which I mentioned earlier. Keep in mind that a key asset for ACS is public trust. The public turned to ACS for reliable information related to cancer. Quantitative research showed that ACS had 98 percent aided and unaided name recognition and a trust level on par with a personal physician. That said, only the marketing people at ACS looked at the brand as an asset until we used these stats and additional research to negotiate the $15 million partnership with Citibank versus their initial offer of $150,000 a year. Citibank knew how many people had been directly or indirectly touched by cancer, and the company believed that the biggest name in the fight against cancer could be part of a recipe to trigger greater use of its credit card. I had no idea how much business partnering with ACS in this way could generate for them, so in an honest effort to learn the value of the brand as an asset in this scenario, I proposed we conduct a test with a small sample of the ACS database. We agreed to base the cost of the license agreement on a projection of the value of the response rate and activation rate for the card. With results in hand, Citibank offered ACS $15 million over five years, along with the ability to place cancer risk information in existing customer communication channels like promotional inserts and newsletters.

If a nonprofit has a unique way of solving a company's problem, that "way" is an asset. Whether you leverage the asset or make the asset available for partnership is another conversation. The point is that you can't negotiate effectively if you don't properly value the asset's worth. Giving assets away happens intentionally when the nonprofit feels that doing so is for the greater good or when a company wants to do so to add more value to a proposal. Unfortunately, nonprofits have unwittingly given away value when they didn't recognize the gift as a valuable asset. Here is a story about that.

The American Cancer Society is known for its scientific research, specifically for spotting and funding young investigator research. ACS has funded over 45 Nobel Prize winners before they achieved broad acclaim. Way before my time with the American Cancer Society, the organization sought to speed the application of research findings in new drugs and treatments for cures. Given that pharmaceutical companies have commercial purposes in the development, production, and sale of medicines, they were a natural partner in accelerating young investigator research. Proven medicines were taken through normal governmental approval processes, produced, and sold by pharmaceutical companies. The companies did speed the availability of new, life-saving drugs. ACS was happy to help, and great good came of it. My point is that by not establishing a clear value for its role in the process, ACS missed out on benefiting monetarily when a pharmaceutical company took a drug to market. In this example, ACS uncovered promising treatments but received no compensation for their role in the eventual product's success.

Growing a nonprofit's perception of its value in different partnership scenarios is essential to effective negotiations and an important key to opening up possibilities for additional partnerships. Recall the Water4 story and how they were phenomenally successful because they took the time to understand the local context. In addition to listening to local needs, Water4 documented a large number of dormant wells in Africa. Over time, nonprofits had built wells which benefited communities until the pumping mechanisms broke. Once a well malfunctioned, money was often not available to buy parts or to fix it. The aid groups had moved on to drill the next well, and the once-productive well now lay abandoned. Water4 saw these as a latent asset and created extraordinary partnerships around them.

"Know your prospective partners' goals, business objectives, and pain points so you know how you can add value. And know the various ways partners can add value to you."

Carol Cone CEO Carol Cone ON PURPOSE, former Chairman and Founder
Cone LLC, and author of *Breakthrough Nonprofit Branding*

Water4's vision is: *Safe water piped to every home and community. Always.* They turn broken wells into productive assets not just by fixing them, but by helping local people make viable, water-based businesses available to local communities. Education, inspiration and microloans are part of the recipe of success. Their work has resulted in farmers growing crops and paying back 100 percent of the loans for seeds and refurbished wells. In a single year, local residents were taking care of their wells themselves. Women created water kiosks on a model similar to phone pay cards. Water4 facilitated the creation of business enterprises from what were abandoned assets. Sustainability and growth resulted by making water profitable for local people. It generated positive ripple effects, addressing other needs, including healthcare access, education, and small business growth. In Ghana, for example, water was provided to 60 health care facilities and 40 schools. In Zambia, the whole country may someday utilize this model.

Successful organizations identify their assets and value them accurately. They also know their weaknesses and prevent those from becoming liabilities during negotiations. Sometimes, you have to bring in an additional partner to offset weaknesses. Remember the three-way partnership between Children International, the local Honduran municipality, and the Catholic church. Each held a strategic piece of the puzzle in delivering food to the poor during the pandemic. Sorting assets like this enables partners to accomplish goals together in ways they could not do independent of each other.

Reflections

What holdings, services, or capabilities does your organization have that are currently considered assets?

Are there any holdings, services or capabilities that are not currently seen as assets internally, but could be seen as assets in a partner's eyes?

How can you determine the value of your assets in your partner's eyes?

CALCULATE YOUR FULL VALUE

—

Determining a quality fit requires accurately sizing up the value and relevance of your prospect's assets and predicting your value to them. The precision and strength of this calculation strengthens your ability to negotiate a fair deal. Data opens the door to productive conversations about leveraging assets beyond a check and a charitable halo.

One of the most powerful stories about value exchange is the partnership between Feeding America and Sam's Club. Sam's Club faced a huge pain point. As described, the company was losing big money by discarding expired food. Feeding America addressed that problem while dramatically increasing the availability of food to those with food insecurity. Over a six-year period, Feeding America became the third-largest hunger relief nonprofit in the United States by establishing similar partnerships with other leading corporations, including Walmart, Kraft, and General Mills. Data made this possible. Feeding America leadership knew the size of this problem for companies and were able to prove they could address it.

Another interesting part of the Feeding America story is how they were able to grow to meet the needs of additional partnerships. They didn't just plow all the new money into existing program activity. They invested in their capacity to move more food and feed more people by expanding their distribution capabilities. As volume increased, they invested a quarter of the Walmart funds on expanding their delivery fleet and adding refrigerated storage. Buying this magnitude of equipment was a courageous investment given the organization's small size at the time. For perspective, Feeding America was raising approximately $20 million a year before they started building corporate alliances to move food to those in need. By 2023, their revenues had grown to $2.9 billion. Again, data backed up their courage.

The availability of quantitative proof of impact continued to fuel Feeding America's growth story. Their success in corporate collaboration led to an impressive partnership with the government, securing them funding through two Farm Bills. The Feeding America mission aligned with a government priority of addressing food insecurity for the homeless, working poor, elderly, and children. The strategic fit could not have been more perfect. The government had money but needed food, supply chain management, and distribution channels, particularly in rural areas. Feeding America had a proven capacity to deliver through their work with corporate partners.

The alignment between Feeding America and entities handling perishable food was easy to see. Proving they could be a relevant partner was harder. Even when that was accomplished, it took more courage and a level of savviness to win staff and board members' support for continued investment in capacity. Had they not invested in expanding capacity, they could not have enlisted additional corporate partners nor won the government contracts.

Here's another story of overcoming difficulties by using data to find a synergistic value exchange between partners. As with Feeding America, this relationship also required courage and commitment to conversation. The Coca-Cola Company and World Wildlife Foundation seem like a natural and iconic fit today. Achieving that beloved relationship and the iconic panda as a symbol of the good they accomplish together was not easy. Let's roll back the clock, learn more of the backstory, and see how they arrived at the beautiful relationship they have today.

"Nonprofits need to understand their value and look at their programs through the eyes of funders as potential investors."

Lance Pierce CEO, NetHope, and former President, Global Development and Head of Partnerships and Sustainable Finance for ADEC Foundation

---

To support a globally expanding business, The Coca-Cola Company and its bottlers needed presence and operations in different countries. They established a double-edged priority, being good corporate citizens while staying true to the quality of their product. Production requires reliable access to a large supply of water. This reality became a challenge, which led to Coca-Cola's commitment to sustainable water sources.

The first Coca-Cola bottling plant in India opened in 1950. Although initially successful, as India's government leaned left over the following years, Coca-Cola came under scrutiny. A point often quoted by politicians at the time was that while only 10 percent of Indians had access to clean water, 90 percent had access to Coca-Cola. The tension around water usage was widespread, but let's look at Carda, India, to understand the local dynamics. Although Coca-Cola was 17th in size among all industries using water in Carda, Coca-Cola had the most prominent brand recognition and received the lion's share of the blame for local water scarcity. This didn't remain a localized issue. Coca-Cola's global reputation took a nosedive from the #1 most admired company to #15. Public impressions certainly impact sales, so the pain wasn't just reputational. The negative media coverage damaged the bottom line, and efforts to manage the public relations fallout were unsuccessful. Coca-Cola eventually closed the bottling plant in Carda, and it remains closed. Even today, the company would have difficulty operating there without local backlash from a continued perception of Coca-Cola as the villain that "robbed the local community of its water."

In light of this history, recommending that Coca-Cola partner with the World Wildlife Fund in an effort to protect water sources was a bold step. The mutual value exchange was not immediately apparent. Without a nod from the top leaders of both organizations, efforts to find a strategic fit might never have happened. Those leaders participated in an introductory meeting in Davos, which went well. That said, it is one thing to have an audacious vision and quite another to bring it into being, even if the top leaders like each other and like an idea.

Internal stakeholders at both organizations felt that the combination of water sustainability and Coke made no sense at all. In particular, naysayers at WWF wondered why they would "get into bed with the enemy" given Coca-Cola's less-than-stellar reputation on the issue. With this initial reception of the partnership, no one would have been surprised if the parties had packed up their bold ideas and gone home.

The good news is that their commitment to listening to each other resulted in mutual appreciation and birthed the improbable. During strategic alignment mapping sessions, the two parties were able to find common ground. Finding this commonality allowed mutual respect to grow. Respect birthed confidence in the idea that a joint approach to addressing their respective goals could be stronger together than going it alone. Water, protected at its source, was one of Coca-Cola's main global initiatives, and safe water was one of WWF's key priorities. Recognizing this led to other rich alignments. Coca-Cola bottlers had strength in advertising and communications expertise at the local level. WWF didn't have resources to fund such expertise at the local level. WWF's key deep knowledge in conservation could help bottling plants with water usage efficiencies. The more openly they talked, the more both sides understood each other and were able to creatively explore the best ideas. In turn, they were able to champion these concepts to other stakeholders.

The success of these alignment sessions led to Coca-Cola, some key European bottlers, and WWF agreeing to a pilot called "Water Savers." The plan spelled out key responsibilities and deliverables for each party. WWF identified ways the bottlers could optimize their water usage with sensitivity to the unique circumstances of each locale. The Coca-Cola Company created an incentive plan for bottlers. The bottler who best improved water efficiency would win an award presented by Coca-Cola's chairman. Everyone recognized the need to work together to manage resources and protect watersheds. The success of this pilot resulted in replicating it at 50 of WWF's 100 global locations and inspired local cooperation across all of Coca-Cola's operating units.

The Coca-Cola Company expanded this approach to partnership building with a $30 million investment over three years. Local bottling plants and their local partners invested even more. For example, in Yangtze, China, HSBC bank contributed $10 million, matching the $10 million from the local Coca-Cola bottler to fund water conservation work there. A team of Coca-Cola representatives and WWF representatives visited the Yangtze River basin, an area critical to panda habitat. They were amazed by the like-mindedness around the mission and support for the work. Affinity grew and even led to good-natured teasing, with locals noting that the Chinese tend to think before they speak while Americans tend to speak before they think! Good continues to grow from this collaboration on many levels and for all partners, as well as for the public. The hard upfront work was well worth it.

Creating strong exchange of value is key to partnership building. The stronger the exchange of value, the bigger the impact for all parties. Persistence, vulnerability, respect, trust, and courage all matter. So does hard data.

Reflections

Nonprofits: what relevance do your assets have in the commercial world?

Companies: have you looked at nonprofit assets to help resolve a business challenge?

NEGOTIATE FOR PROPORTIONAL
VALUE EXCHANGE

—

Beyond the concept of value exchange is the concept of proportional value exchange. This isn't just a nuance. The distinction deserves emphasis since it has been particularly gnarly for both companies and nonprofits. Nonprofits have been known to jump at a dollar figure offered by a company without pausing to see if the offer matches the actual value of their role in the partnership. This is somewhat understandable given that resources are almost never enough to fully fund mission programs.

That is my effort at being polite about what I really see as poor stewardship. Nonprofits owe it to the cause to secure a fair return for what they bring to the table. If an investor walks away rather than talk about fair value, they likely are not the partner you want anyway. It is OK to walk away. Taking the time to arrive at fair value is not only responsible, but it benefits both parties. Remember the ACS story? Pausing to test the value of ACS marks on credit cards grew an initial offer of $150,000 annually to $15 million.

Testing for value doesn't always turn out as brilliantly as in the ACS credit card deal. In addition to potentially turning off an investor, a test could reveal results that don't support collaboration at all. My star at ACS faded a bit after the credit card win when I requested a similar proportional value test with Allstate, a test that didn't turn out as I had hoped. Allstate agreed to research how many more people would agree to a price quote on insurance when the quote triggered a contribution to ACS.

Allstate's prices were competitive, so if their prospects would accept a quote, the company could likely win a new customer. In addition to saving money on insurance, the new customer would support a cure for cancer. The design was similar to the credit card test. It should have worked. Perhaps there was a problem with the demographic of the test, or maybe the communication of the offer was off. Whatever the reason, the numbers told a story that did not justify rolling out the offer. The value to them was deemed so weak that we didn't try to tweak the test. The data tanked the partnership.

"Partnership = strategic, mutual responsibility and gain."

Ann Cramer Civic Leader, Community Volunteer, and Retired
IBM Director Americas, Corporate Citizenship

Had I not insisted on a test in the Allstate discussion, they may have been won over by the strength of the idea and supporting assumptions. They may have been willing to offer a reasonable contribution right away and adjust it based on the conversion of new customers. After all, the data in banking, cereal, and juice was pretty compelling, and the offer was similar. I still stand behind testing the concept because it was right to do. The results prevented disappointment and wasted money from a rollout that would not have even paid for itself. Eventually, in a failed rollout, the numbers would have told the same story that the test revealed. The idea just didn't work with this proposition. We parted with respect for each other, and this was itself valuable. I believe that much good comes from building a reputation for doing the right thing.

Another example of unmet expectations deals with a failed effort to negotiate mutual value. We just couldn't arrive at an agreement that was deemed fair by all. The story is about smoking cessation products, a generic maker of these products, ACS, and Walmart. Spoiler alert: when you have more than two parties talking, negotiations can grow exponentially more complex. This one gave me flashbacks to the time I tried to negotiate a deal with all the television stations in the L.A. market.

Here's the backstory: Another public behavior objective for the American Cancer Society is to help people quit smoking cigarettes. At its height in the 1950s, some 52 percent of Americans smoked. Today, smoking behavior is down to around 12 percent on average, according to the Centers for Disease Control and Prevention. According to the World Health Organization, cigarette smoking is the leading cause of preventable death in the United States, accounting for approximately 443,000 deaths, or one in every five deaths each year.

People start smoking for many reasons, including appetite suppression, calming of nerves, and the desire to belong to a given social group. Regardless of why they start, the addictive nature of the product makes quitting a difficult process for most smokers. The good news when I worked at ACS was that the Food and Drug Administration had just approved products to help people quit smoking. Approved nicotine replacement therapies (NRTs) included gums, skin patches, inhalers, nasal sprays, lozenges, and even vapes. One fly in the marketing effort was that, despite FDA approval, some people lacked confidence in these new products. ACS market research indicated its affiliation could boost public confidence and spur smokers to try these new therapies. Lives could be saved more quickly by speeding the adoption curve for NRTs. With this in mind, ACS placed its name and logo on some of these products with the appropriate educational language, and, as predicted, we saw an uptick in smokers trying these methods to quit smoking.

NicoDerm (patch) and Nicorette (gum) were two NRT products that had permission to use the ACS logo and health message on their packaging. They were produced by SmithKline Beecham, a company which later became GlaxoSmithKline and is now owned by Unilever. Novartis International also came out with generic NRTs, and ACS executed a similar license agreement with them. ACS was passive in all these agreements to avoid being accused of selling the product and triggering another "fun" dialogue with the IRS. ACS retained the right to approve all use of marks and messaging using its name. This was an excellent use of the ACS asset from multiple perspectives: financial, mission, and government oversight.

Proportional value was not straightforward because ACS wanted more than money. The value to the companies was the assumption of increasing sales from the confidence factor ACS provided. The complicating factor was that ACS wanted a non-exclusivity clause. We wanted to strike a similar deal with Novartis for its cheaper generic therapies. Name-brand therapies were expensive, and price was a barrier to lower income smokers who were most likely to suffer the consequences of smoking addiction. ACS didn't want to give an unfair sales advantage to a more expensive product. ACS also wanted customers to know that the cheaper generics were just as safe and as effective as branded products. We also knew that doing this would shorten the life of the value ACS could offer the companies. Our logo on multiple NRTs increased public trust, but in time, the impact on sales from a third party endorsement of science would weaken. Winning partnerships with both companies at the same time was quite an achievement.

"Make sure your partnership strategies are grounded in data and built with a win/win mindset."

Mollye Rhea President and Founder, For Momentum

Now we bring Walmart into the story. With two great NRT product partnerships on board, we saw the potential for an even greater impact on saving lives if we could add a retailer to the mix. Why not pursue the biggest one out there at the time: Walmart? Going big was somewhat influenced by an awareness that our value in the partnership had a shelf life. With Walmart's dedication to bringing the lowest costs to its customers, we felt that Walmart could help us target the smokers least able to afford NRT products. This would save more lives, increase sales of good products, and make Walmart a beloved hero. ACS involvement would be obsolete after a time, but it was worth it. The plan seemed perfect.

I felt certain that Walmart would love this concept. Why not? ACS was a huge brand, well-loved across demographics, and we had proven that the ACS brand could increase sales and public affinity for corporate partners. I ignored the fact that people already loved Walmart. Surely more love would be a good thing.

Novartis believed it was a good idea, too. They agreed to pay for promotional material in the stores. Doing so of course increased the visibility of their generic product over branded products and would increase their sales. Novartis also promised to give a percentage of sales to ACS for products sold through Walmart. ACS, Novartis, Walmart and the customers all would win.

The problem was that I didn't fully grasp the ramifications of a key bit of information I knew about Walmart. The company was famous for negotiating the lowest prices for its customers. It did this by negotiating shrewdly, if not harshly with suppliers. A halo effect from helping save lives from cancer didn't register high on the Walmart team's single-minded savings priority. It was nice, but not a real factor. I was disappointed, but I shouldn't have been. Walmart's staff were professional and clear on their pricing objectives for the customer. They expressed some interest in a three-way partnership if the supplier assumed all the costs related to the promotion. This is where the idea began to unravel. The total cost was too expensive for Novartis, and Walmart saw no significant upside to compromising. The deal fell apart. Perhaps if we had conducted more research to help us address Walmart's driving business objective, we might have negotiated more successfully. Unfortunately, we just could not reach proportional value in Walmart's eyes.

This failure made me remember something important from when we won the Citibank partnership that was missing in the Walmart negotiation. With Citibank, we had internal experts—including our CFO and external volunteer banking experts—

helping us understand the banking and credit card business. They made sure that we were prepared for possible concerns. We were so confident of our concept for Walmart that we didn't engage retail expertise. We thought we knew enough about the retail environment because we had other retail relationships. But we weren't experts, and we could have benefited from that perspective. In truth, experience with one retail environment wasn't sufficient to prepare us for Walmart's unique retail operations. We made a really dumb mistake.

Bruises behind us, let's move on to another story now. The partnership between the Olympics and Coca-Cola is an example of the benefit of taking time to fully understand circumstances and motivations. In this case, the Coca-Cola Company wanted to know what local stakeholders needed to ensure a mutual and fair exchange of value at the local as well as global level. In some countries where Coca-Cola had a presence, they found a creative way to offer local value. As they immersed themselves in local culture, they found ways to be relevant to unique local needs. For example, developing countries have limited resources, but great talent and pride. They could never showcase themselves on a national stage like the Olympics without help. Coca-Cola could make the local dreams come true by paying for teams to train, travel, and participate in the game in exchange for water or bottling permits. All parties—local government, local nonprofits, and Coca-Cola—received something valuable. Whether it was actually proportional in concrete value, I don't know. Sometimes value in the shape of pride and honor balances the scales.

As we close this section, I want to emphasize the fact that value assessments can change. As in the NRT example, ACS's value in building customer confidence in a new medical treatment had a shelf life. Once everyone trusted NRTs, ACS's endorsement of the science would no longer create the desired sales boost. When this happened, the partnership had less value to the companies. Your original assessment of proportional value will change over time and as your relationship evolves. For this reason, savvy partnership builders keep an eye on trends and changes that impact the ongoing value of partnerships. Continually asking yourself about the value equation can position you well when the time comes to renegotiate proportional value to partners.

Failure to stay abreast of how value changes can create missed opportunities. Thinking back to the General Mills/ACS partnership, the initial test was so successful that they wanted to expand the agreement to their other healthy brands. That was wonderful. We loved the idea of having a broader reach of health messaging, so we immediately agreed. In hindsight, I wish I had negotiated access to sales data over a period of time after the start of using ACS marks. ACS may have been due additional value related to General Mills' additional gain. That was likely a missed opportunity.

Reflections

Think of a time you didn't get all you thought a deal was worth. What research could you have done to better position yourself for a fairer exchange of value?

Think of a negotiation that didn't go as planned. What research could have shifted the outcomes of the negotiation?

Chapter 3

———

UNDERSTAND
PARTNER
MOTIVATIONS

Knowing the primary motivation for a prospect's inter-est in working together is key to creating the best stra-tegic alliance. The motivation could be money, credibility, or a greater market share. Maybe it has to do with product or service innovations or help entering a new market. In the last story, General Mill's motivation was impact on pricing strate-gy. As another example described, the Boys and Girls Clubs of America didn't initially understand that their bank partner's priority currency was consumer behavior, specifically credit card usage. You may identify multiple reasons supporting the concept of a specific partnership, but one motivation is likely dominant. Since it may not be immediately apparent, contin-ued conversation can lead you to understand your partner's primary driver. Failing to identify this may impede finding

the strongest strategic alignment. If one party is exclusively interested in impacting sales while the other party talks
only about a charitable benefit, you may never find common
ground. Successful negotiators understand the driving motivation of the other party and speak to how they can impact
that need. Motivation is like currency. In another country, you
have to use their currency to do business.

---

*"Make sure to stay centered on your why before rushing
to what and how...let partnering be the fabric
of the company/nonprofit"*

Mike Siegel former SVP, Marketing, St. Jude Children's Research Hospital

---

Most successful partnership architects take time to carefully discern nuances of need. This allows them to deepen their
relevance to what is important. A rich understanding of need
is the foundation for exploring creative approaches for working
together. It also impacts perceptions of success and sustainability of the relationship. Creating and maintaining strong relevance to partner needs is the backbone of any agreement.

Initiating meetings without knowing what matters most to
a prospective partner is like driving with blinders on. Without
recognizing what is important, you can't know what assets to
offer, and you certainly can't make accurate assessments of value
exchange. Even if you broker a deal under those circumstances,
you won't really know why you secured it. Such a deal is unsus-
tainable. Knowing what really draws the other party to the table

enables you to see the value you have to offer. Relevance to core needs will also enable you to maintain partner interest for as long as that need exists and you are able to support it.

Let's look at several common motivations.

SOCIAL PAYBACKS

We can start with something straightforward to wrap our heads around. In many situations, particularly transactional ones, the motivation between partners appears to be simple. Typically, the nonprofit receives money, and the company improves its philanthropic reputation—a check for a halo. An example is when a company sponsors an event in exchange for the positive positioning as a good corporate citizen. Even in these simple transactions, however, more complex motivations may be at play. This less obvious motivation can actually be more important than the finances or the positive positioning.

Think about the subtle social dynamic behind sponsorship gifts. Perhaps the CEO of one company asks the CEO of another company to support a nonprofit event simply because she supported their event in the past. In essence, the CEO of the other company "owes her." The real value exchange in such circumstances is motivated by a *quid pro quo* between friends and influencers. This courtesy among friends can be the real reason behind the deal.

Experienced event planners have known about social paybacks forever. Tapping this dynamic is why most successful fund-raising events form large host committees composed of well-connected people. Don't be naive and think the purchase of tables or sponsorship packages is primarily about a love for the cause.

These reciprocal paybacks can be powerful forces. Pay attention to them because they can motivate someone to help you. That said, social paybacks aren't likely strong enough to power complex partnerships. To create and sustain the higher level partnerships, you must rely on proven business value.

Reflections

When have you seen social paybacks at play?
When have you used these reciprocal paybacks?

INFLUENCE

In this section, we'll talk about the power of influence as a political force and also as a key motivator in negotiations. Whether such influence is internal or external in nature, it can positively or negatively impact relationships. Like social paybacks, this kind of influence might not have much to do with partners' strategies or any direct business motivation for working together. Partnership dynamics can grow exponentially more complicated when this big sister of social paybacks joins the fray.

Political maneuverings sometimes share the same premise as social paybacks, but they can involve several people at once and use enticements as well as threats. The stakes can be higher, too. With all this in mind, it is no wonder that Washington insiders refer to "how the sausage is made" to describe hammering out legislative deals. To keep the book from straying off course, we won't talk about the strange bedfellows that can arise when politicians need to partner with those who aren't normally perceived as allies or even friends. If your partnership has the misfortune of becoming embroiled with government or organizational politics, tread carefully.

The next story demonstrates the pressure and impact that can color a partner's reality when political factors arise. Let's examine AT&T's experience when the College Football Hall of Fame was deciding which major city to call its home. We need some backstory to understand how politics complicated the company's ability to strategically align. AT&T's headquarters is in Dallas, while the department responsible for all the company's advertising buys, sponsorships, and philanthropic investments was led out of Atlanta. The Hall of Fame was seen as a magnet for money and tourism, so the municipal governments and corporate leadership in both cities wanted the Hall of Fame. Major companies were courted for their financial support to help land the deal. Everyone believed it would positively impact the local economy.

AT&T felt intense pressure to support bids in Atlanta and in Dallas. The company was looking forward to supporting the effort in whichever city the Hall of Fame's leadership eventually chose. It wasn't directly related to AT&T's strategy for philanthropic investment, but it was important to them to be viewed as a good corporate partner by the local governments. This perception could impact other business objectives.

Given the sensitivity of local politics and perceptions

around support of the bids, the head of AT&T philanthropic investment in Atlanta had to be neutral as the political process played out. To avoid any semblance of favoritism, AT&T would not utter an official word until one city was actually selected by the Hall of Fame. AT&T still needed, however, to engage with local leaders and philanthropic partners in each city on other topics. Given the buzz around the competition for the Hall of Fame, avoiding this deliberation proved difficult. Unfortunately, an effort to explain AT&T's balancing act to a nonprofit leader in the Atlanta area was misconstrued as advance support for Atlanta. Worse, this leader innocently shared his understanding of AT&T's intent to fund Atlanta's effort to attract the Hall of Fame in a public forum. This reverberated quickly and created an internal backlash at AT&T. This comment unfortunately resulted in delaying AT&T's ability to invest in the Football Hall of Fame for over a year.

Another place to see this kind of influence play out is wherever you have a Convention Visitor Bureau (CVB) or Chamber of Commerce. These entities have no authority to make anyone do anything, but their mission is to attract businesses and grow local economies. As such, they have a vested interest in making their cities appealing while honoring unique aspects of the cities and their surrounding areas.

Atlanta, for example, is a proud city. It is also a complex jumble of motives, dreams, and opportunities spiced up with diverse communities who are living out of different contexts, histories, and current experiences. That was a mouthful and every bit of it true. Add to that, as in all cities, modern media reinforces individuals' opinions multiple times a day with sophisticated logarithms that serve up content based on what we've "liked." Opinions are not just formed but reinforced constantly—and not always with facts. This dynamic affects city and corporate leaders as much as the everyday person on the street. In this landscape, all kinds of opinions can feel rock solid before any discourse even begins. Such is the nature of the influence that is as present as the air we breathe.

With all the noise mentioned above in play, a special kind of leadership is required to listen for, articulate, and amplify common ground. More than your average dose of charisma is needed. Such leaders pay attention and seek to validate all perspectives. They remain on message and steer toward a common way forward on any given issue. Sometimes this dance plays out in traditional or social media, but with regard to high level influencers, it also percolates within small circles of decision-makers. Often, it plays out in both. In this league of influence, keen people skills, focus, and stamina allow successful partnership builders to marshal support for their desired outcomes.

This next story regarding the power of influence involves the Visitors' Bureau, corporate community, government, and two nonprofits in Atlanta. Remember what I said about complexity increasing with the number of players involved? We are on steroids now. The community leadership conversation accelerated as Atlanta's massive aquarium project neared completion. The corporate and political leadership of Atlanta anticipated that the attraction would be a wonderful jewel in the city's crown, one that would boost tourism and its related revenue. On this, everyone agreed.

A major concern surfaced about the Atlanta Mission, a facility that provides shelter, food, and other assistance to the city's homeless. The Mission was located next door to the aquarium site. Some leaders expressed concern about the difficult street scene visitors departing from the aquarium would encounter. People in dire need gathered all around the Mission. Some thought that such a sight could tarnish visitors' impression of the city. To address this perceived threat, leaders considered relocating the Mission to another part of downtown. Such a decision, however, would leave desperate people who could not relocate themselves without critical resources to survive.

Moving the Mission would upend a successful program, and a new location would not remove the problem: the people in need. This uncomfortable fact was a key piece of information that helped pave common ground. A better understanding of homelessness created room for a more humane solution to surface. The new idea bred renewed partnership between corporate interests, city interests, and the Mission, which ultimately benefited both tourism and homeless advocacy interests. The Mission stayed in its location next to the aquarium, but it did not remain the same. With an influx of corporate support and the advocacy of then mayor Shirley Franklin, the Mission received funds to strengthen its programs and facility appearance. It became even more of a success story and not a blight. Great leadership fueled a positive, collective solution, pushed it to a tipping point, and then secured the necessary resources for it.

In complex situations like this, more was going on than just the merging of political, economic, and charitable motivations.

The power of personal experience can override all that. The mayor's support and energy to influence this debate had roots deeper than her commitment to all of Atlanta's citizens. Franklin's father had himself faced homelessness and had benefited in large part from the kind of assistance offered by the Atlanta Mission. She deeply believed this path was good. Her personal connection lended the negotiation more purity of cause. Even when not stated explicitly, this factored heavily in her ability to influence others.

One last example of the power of influence comes from early in my career. I was working for the Trident United Way on a pilot program to explore a new way to reduce repeat criminal behavior among minors. The position was funded by a combination of government grants and United Way. The premise was that kids would be better off if they had a chance to work off their crimes rather than being locked up or put on probation. Incarceration was rarely a rehabilitative experience for youth, and being one of some fifty kids assigned to a probation officer didn't guarantee much personalized intervention.

The pilot program was one of three such tests in the country. The budget was tiny, and, as I mentioned earlier, I was hired in part because I had been a TV weather broadcaster in college and that was considered "close enough" to the art of public relations to justify me doing two roles: working with the kids and handling PR. I didn't really know anything about public relations work, but my friends did, and they also knew influential people in the media. By informally engaging my friends, I was able to meet local decision-makers and stoke interest in this novel test. These advocates made it possible to secure interviews for the program's executive director, workplace supervisors, and the kids on TV and radio, as well as in newspaper outlets. (No social media back then!)

After eighteen months, government representatives came to evaluate the pilot's targeted measures for success. One of those was public opinion of the program. The research showed 52 percent public awareness and a positive opinion of the program. This was remarkable given that the program didn't exist a year and a half prior to the research. But really, we succeeded because we were able to galvanize the interest of multiple influencers to address something they all had in common: a concern for kids.

Working at United Way offered me many opportunities to continue learning about how and why people come together for mutual benefit. Specifically, the experience taught me the importance of focusing on key motivations. This story is also about media support, but I didn't initially have a strong value exchange for the media. The United Way communications committee and I decided we needed to do something unique to engage more people with the great nonprofits we funded. The thinking was that if people participated with our funded agencies in a fun way, they would be more inclined to support funding them. With plenty of water enthusiasts in the area, we decided to orchestrate a water race with homemade rafts. Staff from United Way, their funded programs, and employees from area companies built rafts. Over a hundred homemade crafts with eight-person crews entered the race. Each team also recruited cheering squads to celebrate on land at the finish line. The event was generating tons of excitement.

Logistics were not easy. In addition to the normal event planning activities, this one required approvals from local government and Coast Guard oversight for safety. The work was complicated, but everything was going swimmingly. . . except for media support. They were interested in day-of-event coverage, but we wanted more. We were looking for promotions, feature stories, and sponsorship.

The lukewarm reception from the media puzzled me. This was going to be a fun, well-attended event supporting all kinds of good causes. Local media should love it. We enthusiastically shared our well-rehearsed pitch in front of the right decision-makers. Hmmm. They were ever so nice to us, but the answer was a "no, thank you." I remember repeating how many new people would be supporting all the great programs and how much positive impact this event would have in our community. I told them how many attendees we expected, how much fun it would be, and how safety would be a priority. I thought it would be a terrific deal for them.

That was the issue. The plan only sounded fantastic to me and our committee. I wasn't addressing what really motivated the media. One of the facts I missed was that hordes of nonprofits approached the media every day with fantastic ideas. They couldn't say yes to every group, and supporting such charitable events generally ignited a wave of even more requests.

With the weight of rejection and my head downcast, I went to my boss and apologized. I had put on my best smile and tried, but I had failed to win media support. Our dream for this event wasn't going to pay off like we hoped because the media weren't signing on. We would have plenty of attendees, but the broader exposure wasn't in the cards. He listened kindly and then asked me what I had asked the media to do. This seemed a little insulting to me, but I replied that I had asked them to sponsor the event and added that it was a very good deal for them. I honestly still didn't understand why I was rejected or how I could change their minds.

My boss gave me advice I've never forgotten. He pushed me to consider what newspapers and radio stations really cared about, what really motivated them. After some back and forth, it dawned on me that obviously what allows the media to succeed in business is revenue. And their revenue came from advertisers. These decision-makers, whom I had begun to cast in my heart as uncaring, just needed something more. If I wanted their support, I had to connect to what really drove them. Unfortunately, I didn't have money to buy advertising.

My ever-patient boss, Charlie Fruit, then invited me to think about whether the companies represented on our board were current advertisers with the TV stations, radio stations, and newspapers that I had approached. Like many United Ways, we had heavy corporate hitters on our board of directors who had healthy advertising budgets. Lightbulbs started turning on for me. Charlie helped me connect with several members of our board, some of whom agreed to contribute to an advertising pool to buy ads for the event. They were also willing to sponsor and attend a VIP reception before the event. When I returned to the media with advertising dollars in hand and the opportunity for them to mingle with potential new advertising buyers, they were much more interested. They became the media partners we were hoping for and even matched the advertising space committed by our board members. The opportunity for new advertising revenue was the motivation they needed. The stations and newspapers had plenty of opportunities to "look good" to viewers or advertisers. Only when we began to talk their language, honor their business needs, and bring them a clear and powerful value proposition did the improbable become probable.

Reflections

How have governmental or organizational politics influenced your partnerships?

How did you navigate these kinds of influences?

What strategies would you continue to use, and what would you never use again?

CONSUMER BEHAVIOR

Companies and nonprofits also share the need to influence consumer behavior, and they do so by focusing on market segments with relevant propositions. The two kinds of consumer markets that companies and nonprofits want to influence are business-to-business or business-to-consumer. Companies can sell to other companies, to individual consumers, or to both. Likewise, nonprofits have revenue models engaging entities like companies and foundations, and they target individuals. It is all business. To be successful, corporate and nonprofit businesses need individuals or other entities to invest in their various propositions for value. At the end of the day, a partner's mind is always occupied to some degree with driving people's behavior. Awareness of products and services, markets, reputation, price, and competition are all parts of the equation. How partners relate to the factors that influence consumer behavior is where the magic for powerful partnerships lies. The ability to impact consumer behavior is a key currency for partner discussions.

Where nonprofits are concerned, the specific consumer behaviors are broader than persuading companies and individuals to part with money. They also need to influence behaviors such as convincing people to wear seatbelts, get cancer tests, plant trees, or any number of other actions related to making the planet a better, healthier place for all of us. For every nonprofit consumer behavior desired, an array of companies exist who share interest in the same behaviors. We've talked about companies that sell juice, fruit, and cereals and how they can match for nonprofits that want people to eat healthily and exercise to reduce risks of disease. Showing that you understand consumer behavior and that you are relevant to it from a business perspective will put you ahead of others in crafting successful deals.

When I talked about the relationship between General Mills and the American Cancer Society (ACS), I was taken seriously because I quickly established relevance to their need for more people to buy cereal and to pay more for it. ACS could dramatically influence this consumer behavior, and that was the dominant factor for General Mills.

Here is a very different scenario regarding consumer behavior, one that underscores how multiple motivations can influence prospective partnerships. One driver of interest is almost always dominant, but it is rarely that simple. Adding to the complexity, the dominant reason one entity is interested may not explain their potential partner's interest. Keep sight of what you need as you strive to find common ground with your potential partner. You'll have an easier time if you are upfront about your needs as you listen to your prospective partner's reasons for coming to the table. Pausing to periodically reiterate what you hear and how you relate to their needs is also a good way to keep moving forward toward mutual gain.

"Market segmentation represents a rational and more precise adjustment of product and marketing effort to consumer requirements."

Wendell R. Smith *Journal of Marketing,* 1956

Those points were important factors in Susan G. Komen for the Cure's aim to boost breast cancer survival in the Middle East. Komen knew they could replicate Western success in saving lives if they could convince women in this region to schedule mammograms. If found early, the disease could be successfully treated. Seemingly simple, this pragmatic approach to consumer behavior ran afoul of cultural and religious beliefs. In this region, admitting that you had breast cancer was taboo. Doing so would create social stigma not only for the patient, but also for her family—possibly jeopardizing a daughter's chances for marriage. Given this, women would rather not know they had cancer in the first place. The social consequence of having cancer seemed to be an immovable barrier. Only one entity could really change this: the powerful voice of the country's top influencer could initiate a change in women's opinions and behavior.

Hala Moddelmog, then CEO for Komen, and U.S. First Lady Laura Bush met with King Abdul of Saudi Arabia to discuss the needless loss of women's lives in his country. A king has many priorities for his country, but his heart was moved by the preventable loss of life. After this conversation, King Abdul purposefully said the words "breast cancer" out loud in a public forum to begin to reverse the culture of silence. This only happened because two brilliant women aligned with the leader's heart for his people. When he used his influence to shift the culture, women listened, and this saved lives.

Another example of Komen's keen understanding of consumer behavior as a common motivation for partnership comes from their work to save Native American women's lives. This culture also avoided talking about breast cancer, but they did so because of their religious understanding. The prevailing belief was that burial of a deceased one's whole body was necessary for the person to enter heaven. A mastectomy prevented the whole body from being buried. Women chose a horrible death in order to honor their faith. The desire to go to heaven conflicted with the goal of saving lives from breast cancer.

Komen again needed a credible voice to help revise the prevailing spiritual narrative. Faith leaders were the only ones who could do this. Thankfully, these leaders were motivated to partner out of duty to their faith and compassion for their followers. They saved lives by assuring women that cancer treatment would not cost them their souls. Believing their faith leaders, women started getting screened. The shift in women's behavior came by focusing on who could most influentially carry the message.

A key takeaway for the reader here is to make sure you understand the driving factors influencing the behaviors you want to create. Only then is it possible to determine what might impact the behavior and which partners you need to help you do it. Once you know that, you have to think about why the prospective partner would agree to work with you. That "why" reveals the reason or motivation they may have for partnering with you. In the examples just mentioned, the motivations were the same: all parties genuinely wanted to save lives.

One note of caution. Focusing on a single reason a prospect may want to partner with you can ultimately weaken your position. Definitely focus your attention on the dominant motivation, but consider conferring with others as you proceed. Addressing only one motivation is similar to working with only one tool in your toolbelt, having a hammer and seeing everything as a nail. If you address as many important factors as you can, you become relevant to the broader tapestry of what a partner deems important. For example, if you view nonprofits as beneficiaries which only need money or volunteers, you'll only see a fraction of what is possible. You won't see their assets or their ability to influence behaviors. Such a myopic view will prevent you from envisioning greater opportunities. Those of you representing nonprofits must avoid viewing companies purely as moneybags. Dig deeper. Understand what makes a company tick, and make yourself relevant to their business needs.

Reflections ───────────────────────────

Think of a time when partner discussions evolved so smoothly
that they seemed to have a life of their own. What was
present? Did you know what each other needed, and did you
find common ground on how to do something meaningful
together?

Think of times when partner discussions were hard. Why were
they hard? Did you have adequate mutual value to discuss?

───────────────────────────────────────

CAPACITIES

Several of the stories I've shared so far relate to a partner's
need for additional capability beyond money or reputation. Unilever needed a nonprofit partner with supply chain expertise to
deliver pallets of Vaseline to disaster relief sites. Sam's Clubs
needed a distribution solution to its perishable food dilemma.
Children International in Honduras needed to transport emergency food supplies to hungry families. All these organizations
sought strategic partners to fill their capacity gaps.

I believe partnerships built from specific needs hold the
potential to be the strongest and most sustainable of all. That is
as long as the partners remain relevant to each other's business
goals. For example, if Sam's Club had decided to build out its
own logistics to distribute food to food banks through its own
nonprofit, they would no longer need Feeding America. That
scenario was highly improbable given the resources required
to build what Feeding America could already do so well. In the

other example, if CI bought its own trucks, they wouldn't have needed local municipalities to help with transportation. If a motivating need disappears, so does a partnership built solely around that need. Essentially, what is no longer relevant must be sunset.

A compelling need can help launch a partnership, but identifying ongoing points of relevance sustains relationships. Schedule regular opportunities with your partners to explore a diverse array of ideas for building business success or for addressing specific challenges.

Utilize asset mapping and key questions to continually reflect on the business you are in. Feeding America could have seen themselves as only in the business of providing food to the food insecure. Indeed, they do that well, but they are also in the transportation business. By recognizing that capability and its potential value to companies like Sam's Club, they were able to initiate partnerships with a variety of companies who needed a solution to dumping perishable food.

Reflections

What businesses are you in? What capabilities do you have?

How might asset mapping help you identify a match between your capabilities and a prospective partner's need?

Of the partners that could use your organization's core capabilities, what do they have that could be of value to you? What is the value exchange?

MARKET ACCESS

Entering new markets with an established product or service can be challenging and expensive. So can the introduction of new products and services in existing markets. Speeding the phases related to either proposition will hit the bottom line in a good way, and partnerships can help. The key is to partner with an already respected entity in the desired market. This strategy works whether the "markets" are defined geographically, psychographically, or behaviorally as long as you can show alignment with your prospective partner's driving goals.

Several of our stories have dealt with this motivation. When pharmaceutical companies wanted to attract smokers to their smoking cessation products, they chose to partner with ACS to establish greater credibility for their new products. Similarly, when Elongate sought to be seen as more philanthropic in crypto communities, they aligned with Children International because CI was one of the few nonprofits that had achieved visibility in crypto communities and was valued for its impact on reducing childhood poverty. Lastly, when Citibank wanted to offer a credit card to the cancer community, they chose to work with the American Cancer Society. With ACS, Citibank could imbue more emotional value for those affected by cancer.

A new example of the motivation around product launch and market entry involves Kohler and World Vision. Kohler is a 150-year-old company with a wide range of products for the kitchen and bathroom. They have a presence in forty-five countries and a commitment to leaving the world better than they found it. The numerous awards they've received from the U.S.

Environmental Protection Agency is a testament to this conviction. They recently received the Water Sense Sustained Excellence Award for the ninth time, most recently for their efforts and innovation in water efficiency and plumbing. Kohler is ranked 47th in the EPA's 2023 Green Power Partnership list of the largest consumers of renewable power. World Vision is one of Kohler's many impressive partners, and safe water is one of World Vision's key strategic priorities for reducing poverty. This story is about advancing an innovative solution to clean water in India, a country where most of its citizens do not have easy access to safe water. The story is also about a new product launch.

Kohler developed an in-home water purification product that was lightweight, able to hold several gallons of water, and easy to use. They wanted to test this product in select Indian markets where they already had a presence. If the testing succeeded, they planned to sell the units and donate purification products to the poor. This was consistent with the company persona of doing well by doing good. To move forward, Kohler needed a reputable partner who knew about safe water and local needs. By distributing some of the units through World Vision, Kohler could grow its reputation as a caring company and build product awareness. The idea addressed an enlightened corporate self interest while creating movement for the nonprofit's mission. The prospective partners were well aligned.

Whether the company or the nonprofit starts the conversation about joining forces, the key questions to success are the same. First, they need to know exactly what they need from each other to be successful. Then they can calculate a value for what each is bringing to the partnership. Finally, before moving forward, they must answer the question of how beneficiaries and customers benefit, too.

Reflections

What are your priority markets (demographic, psychographic, behavioral)? Which of your partners or prospective partners share your market focus?

How might you assist a partner—or receive assistance—in a given market?

Chapter 4

BUILD
INTERNAL
PARTNERSHIPS

So much of the current thinking about partnership building focuses on preparing for and artfully executing negotiations to maximize your side's benefit. This book is no exception. There is, however, another dynamic to address that can buoy—or sink—your efforts before you even begin talking to a partner. The internal workings of an organization can accelerate or hamper the ability to create and sustain partnerships. This is true of profit and nonprofit entities alike. Personally, I often found it easier to "sell" partnership concepts externally than internally.

The root of the challenge involves the multitude of internal stakeholders involved in approving and fulfilling partnership agreements. Each of them has unique and sometimes shifting needs. If these needs aren't addressed or if partnership requirements run counter to them, it can jeopardize external partner agreements. In essence, multiple internal stakeholders have to be satisfied with each partnership negotiation, a task that sometimes feels like herding cats.

Another challenge in keeping internal parties supportive of partnerships is that each partnership is different. This uniqueness can require seeking buy-in every time a new partner opportunity develops. One partnership might involve mobilizing action by local staff, whereas another might require establishing a deep knowledge of an unfamiliar business or revenue model. Different products, programs, or services could be involved. The communications staff always needs to be involved in work with partner organizations so that both entities are in sync regarding external messaging. This can necessitate understanding new arenas of business while being alert for possible PR pitfalls. It is a time-consuming task that never ends. The same issue can face legal and finance teams too. There is little about complex partnerships that is turnkey. All this is said to emphasize the point that negotiation skills and people skills are important to securing needed internal support in co-creating and maintaining partnerships. You can not build partnerships without all these support services in place.

Internal stakeholders' complex needs affect their openness to new partnerships. Obviously, new partnerships mean more work. Even if internal stakeholders love the idea of partnerships, limited resources, conflicts of interest, or pure dislike for a given partner can create resistance.

A good example of managing internal needs came from Zoo Atlanta. The CEO, Raymond King, and his team have built numerous successful partnerships with local companies by approaching these opportunities as business relationships. Their success is in great part attributable to King's belief that alliances with companies can't be unilaterally negotiated and executed by one person. This story demonstrates his belief in bringing along the whole organization as partnerships develop. Doing so creates cohesion and addresses internal difficulties before they can negatively impact the partner's experience.

"Human resources are like natural resources; they're often buried deep. You have to go looking for them; they're not just lying around on the surface."

Ken Robinson author and advisor

In this case, the zoo staff wasn't initially keen on pursuing corporate engagements. They felt that they were being asked to monetize the animals. This felt downright distasteful to zookeepers who are passionate about animals and didn't want to see them exploited. The aversion was strong and had the potential for galvanizing negative feelings for partnerships. These staff were essential to the corporate customer experience, and they were not enthused about this kind of corporate engagement. Efforts to partner weren't looking good.

Part of the problem was language. Zookeepers were turned off by words like *monetizing* and *capital assets,* so King abandoned the "business speak." More importantly, he listened to their concerns and acted on what he heard. This was a wise move, and everyone in the partnership business could benefit from doing so. King learned that the zookeepers really cared about securing more resources to build better animal habitats. They identified specific investments that would help the animals thrive. Incorporating the zookeepers' perspective and keeping them in the loop as he created a corporate engagement strategy demonstrated his genuine concern for the animals and his staff. His approach generated common ground and mutual respect. With this foundation, the zookeepers supported corporate partnerships as a new way of soliciting desperately-needed funds for habitats.

CREATE AN INCLUSIVE TEAM
—

A core partnership development team includes people responsible for cultivating, negotiating, and stewarding partnerships. This team handles the daily activities of good partnership work, but team members can't do their job without the support of other key internal stakeholders. Relationship management won't blossom without prospect research, reliable IT systems, and responsive legal, finance, and communications services. Add to that the involvement of program and service staff with the bookends of C-suite and local community support. Partnership building is essentially a business within a business. All internal stakeholders need to view themselves as part of the team. I found it helpful to structure the core partnership team as an internal client of service departments with the overarching premise of reciprocal value. Doing well at partnership work could benefit everyone. This was also the culture achieved by Zoo Atlanta. Everyone became genuinely invested in the idea of corporate engagement.

The ideal core team responsible for partnerships also has a visionary leader with strong people skills. This person acts as a "player coach" for the team. He or she deals externally with partners, but also negotiates and promotes internal support for the business of partnership-building, both as a broad concept and for specific deals. But a leader like that isn't all that is required. Everything can fall like a house of cards without strong administrative support and project management skills. The real measure of an optimal team is found beyond checking boxes of skill sets and defining individuals' roles on organizational charts. Ultimately, the most successful teams have passion and a genuine commitment to each other and the greater collective outcome.

Ask yourself if your core team has the following characteristics:

- High trust of each other in an atmosphere of healthy competition
- Inclusive and respectful approach to securing internal services and support
- Authentic, honest, and timely communication all the time
- Active appreciation for different styles, approaches, and experiences
- Collective development of individual and team goals with common ownership of all goals
- Strong individual and team incentives, both monetary and non-monetary

- Steady commitment to ongoing learning
- Deep passion for the cause, the partners (internal and external), and the outcomes

If you have identified these characteristics in your team, you will surpass normal expectations for team ROI. And it will be fun!

Let's move beyond the formation and chemistry of the immediate group responsible for delivering partnerships. As noted, the very nature of partnerships requires skill sets that don't all naturally reside in one department. For example, I have never seen legal and financial services embedded in a core partnership team. All of the internal stakeholder departments must see themselves as part of the overall partnership business. They must be accountable for their part in closing deals and maintaining relationships. In order to steward internal partners well, keep these keys to engaging internal stakeholders in mind:

- Early involvement of all service departments in any new deal (no surprises)
- Negotiation of resources and deliverables unique to each deal
- Shared praise for wins
- Protection from blame when something goes wrong
- Celebration
- Strong, ongoing communication

The shortlist of internal stakeholders who are not on your core team starts with the C-suite. If the top leadership isn't passionate about partnership building, you'll likely have difficulty garnering the resources needed for successful operations. You also need the CEO to participate passionately at key milestones in the cultivation, solicitation, and stewardship process. Other priority areas of support include legal and financial departments due to the potential risks involving money and other assets. Normally, legal and financial departments have sign-off responsibilities before deals can be finalized. This is essential within reason (more on that later). Next, communications and public relations departments are customarily essential to any partnership, and not just the leadership of the departments. Executional staff need to be in the loop from the beginning and have the necessary resources. They may love you and your concept for a partnership, but if you are not a priority for them, you will encounter problems. Next, if your partnership concept involves a product, program, or service line, you need them to buy in and support the partnership, too. Most importantly, if your deal involves local activation, your regional or local operations staff is absolutely essential.

Remember all the keys to successfully engaging internal stakeholders. I listed them, but they deserve a little more ink. The first one is to involve the internal stakeholders early in the process. Don't surprise them with last-minute requests. If you see signs hung in a support department that say something like "Your urgency isn't my emergency," you likely have work to do regarding early engagement and collaborative planning. Next, always share the glory when a partnership is successful. If people feel like they play a role in the win, but are unsung heroes, you'll have trouble expecting their whole-hearted dedication later.

The next one might sound a little odd, but you need to shield your core team and internal partners from blame when hiccups arise. We've all experienced glory grabbing around successes. As they say, success has many fathers and mothers, but failure has none. No one wants to raise their hand and claim failure. Usually, partnerships fail for multiple reasons. Instead of pointing fingers at faults, be the leader who steps forward to own the flop and the disappointment. Throw no one under the bus. Shine a light on what worked well. Detail the lessons learned and what is needed to succeed moving forward.

Finally, celebrate together. Be the fun group! Invite everyone to the party and hug them tight. OK, some people hate being hugged. I'm a hugger—it's part of my charm. I have found that if you threaten to hug a hug-hater but don't actually do it, you'll get a smile that will warm your heart and theirs.

If possible, regularly ask top leadership to express their support for partnership building along with the expectation that all internal stakeholders prioritize it. This prevents you from having to threaten to bring in the big guns if someone isn't fulfilling their role or playing nice.

Even after employing these keys, you may find yourself held hostage by one group which, for reasons very important to them, is not helping the cause. This is when we return to learning what is important to them to determine what is behind their resistance. Don't immediately complain to the boss. Learning what is going on with them, you can usually find a way to bring them back into the fold. As with external partners, you address their needs—and pain points—as you negotiate service support. This is why the art of internal partnership building is a necessary prerequisite to building external relationships.

Time for a story. I joined World Vision to build a corporate engagement team focused on monetary investments. They had a robust operation focused on securing product donations. My team would walk alongside that operation. I had top leadership support, key department support, and a mature sales team. I assumed we also had warm leads thanks to the product team's existing corporate relationships. This assumption, that product engagement reps would happily provide introductions for my team, proved to be problematic. The product team didn't have any real incentive to open doors for us. In fact, they saw facilitating such introductions as undercutting their own value. I faltered by not ensuring that the product team felt essential to the success of the cash team. Had I properly applauded that team's role in this new business unit, they might have responded more positively. More than that, I should have worked out incentives benefiting those who made introductions that produced successful business relationships. This could have essentially made my talk about internal partnership real to them.

Full confession: that wasn't my only stumble with regard to internal dynamics at World Vision. At the time, World Vision's website spoke to child sponsorship conversations, not corporate conversations. Child sponsorship generated the lion's share of the organization's revenue. The digital team had clear marching orders to gear the site to sponsorships. Placing corporate engagement on the homepage was seen as a distraction for donors as well as a revenue drain. The web staff did what they felt they could, but corporate engagement was essentially buried deep in the website. A smarter move would have been for me to wait to engage companies until we had a clearer website strategy. This is just one example of making sure C-suite support translates into the essential departmental support of partnership building.

I thought I could overcome the website weakness with informative in-person meetings because my team had been able to do this where we had existing relationships. This flawed thinking became apparent when we approached companies who were unfamiliar with World Vision. Websites are part of the basic due diligence that companies and nonprofits use to vet opportunities before investing much time on them. It wasn't until a lost opportunity with MetLife that I prioritized IT's role.

I knew the decision-maker at MetLife and had successfully gained support from them while at the American Cancer Society. Thinking that was enough to bypass the website weakness, I reached out to explore how World Vision aligned with their foundation's strategies. I was granted the meeting, but within a day, the invitation was withdrawn. It felt like a roller coaster. The MetLife leader had naturally asked her staff to research World Vision in preparation for our meeting. While browsing our website, all they saw was child sponsorship opportunities, and this was not a fit for the company. Metlife's leader was a busy person and trusted her staff's assessment. Sadly, I didn't get a second chance to redeem this poor first impression. I burned an opportunity to build a mutually beneficial relationship.

Reflections

Does your core team have all the necessary characteristics of success?

Do you have C-suite passion and support for partnership-building?

Do you devote time to stewarding relationships with internal stakeholders whose services are essential to partnership-building?

Are there any fence-mending or relationship development activities needed with any of the key internal stakeholder departments so that they not only can but also want to support you?

PUSH NORMS

Bear with me for a second. I'm going to whisper to the non-profits for a moment. Nonprofits compete fiercely for corporate engagement. The deluge of requests for support is what drives many companies to develop charitable selection criteria in the first place. As I've noted, clear criteria for partner selection saves time and creates a greater impact for both parties. Even so, the playing field is crowded, and you may or may not be a fit. One way to deal with this is to follow innovation and entrepreneurs into less crowded fields. This can be risky, and it isn't the norm.

Going where others aren't requires that you think courageously and adopt a mindset of what marketers call "first movers." These leaders enter new markets or introduce new products or services first. If it works, they win big and crowds usually follow. For partnership building, this requires not only courage within the partnership team, but also a certain level of tolerance for risk by senior management. Sometimes, even the board of directors needs to feel comfortable. Three examples of this are celebrity endorsements, cryptocurrency, and gaming. If you have a risk-averse organization, feel free to skip the rest of this section.

Opportunities involving unfamiliar businesses, communities, or cultures take time for people to embrace. In some cases, about the time leaders begin to grow comfortable with the novelty, the market changes or technology upends the norm. Technology has spurred phenomenal change at an accelerating pace. Staying abreast of trends in businesses, communities, and media channels is challenging, but it can help you find opportunities that those who focus on a single point in time can't see.

My first story is about celebrities and internal stakeholders applying old school information to a new opportunity. For context, when I worked at the American Cancer Society, we had both success stories and war stories about working with celebrities. The difficult situations included everything from personal demands like removing brown M&Ms from a candy bowl to drawing the organization into controversy because of off-the-cuff remarks or imprudent behavior. These experiences led ACS to adopt policies to guide its work with celebrities. One of these guidelines prohibited paying for celebrity endorsements.

Fast forward: ACS has a new sports marketing leader, a dynamic individual who is up to date on the latest trends in digital media. Social media endorsements have become a thriving business that generates results. Celebrities are just as unpredictable as they used to be, but social media moves at its own pace. Controversy can be quickly buried by new events. Public memory can be short, and some might say that the bar is lower for appropriate comments and online decorum. All that said, just one post from a celebrity with a large following can shift opinions and spur revenue. Unfortunately, ACS's old policy created a roadblock for what is now a widely accepted practice. The old guard felt it was still too risky to embrace this new approach to influencing behavior.

As time passes, perhaps this new way of engaging with celebrities will become more comfortable. In the meantime, those who can move forward will find media companies eager to help leverage celebrity influence effectively. Some of them focus exclusively on brokering deals with social media influencers. OpenDorse is one such agency that matches nonprofit donor profiles with sports celebrities. They also monitor celebrity performance against specific contractual agreements so companies and nonprofits can measure the ROI of their investment. The current technology also allows for quick action if a celebrity should create unacceptable "noise." Failing to harness the power of influencers is a huge missed opportunity.

When building organizational support for something new, timing can be all-important. An easy example is aligning with budget cycles. Requesting resources after the budget is approved provides an easy reason to reject an idea—the money is no longer available. Another timing consideration is being nimble enough to ride news cycles when they can benefit you.

Media coverage of the ups and downs of cryptocurrency helped move this next idea along.

Cryptocurrency communities grew globally in what seemed like a blink of an eye. Many nonprofits were skeptical of entering this new market because they didn't know enough and didn't trust the crypto ecosystem itself. The wild gyrations in the value of cryptocurrency didn't help matters. Add to that a fear of bad actors in this space, and you have heads shaking before you say much of anything. Nonprofits are generally cautious entities, particularly their legal and financial advisors. In 2017, the value of cryptocurrency grew too big to ignore, and more than a few crypto investors made huge fortunes. Some of these individuals sought to donate philanthropically a portion of their windfalls. In 2019, UNICEF became the first UN organization to receive, hold, and redistribute cryptocurrency. Their foray spurred other nonprofits to become bolder and to seek out experts to help them engage safely.

Children International (CI) was another early adopter in cryptocurrency. They had tested the crypto water years before the new wave arrived. Although their first experiment fell short, they preserved the capability to accept cryptocurrency. Equally important, they didn't let the sting of past failure prevent them from testing again. CI prides itself as a learning organization, and this was certainly an example of that mindset.

Good timing came into play in two ways. As the media was covering the spike in cryptocurrency, I happened to meet Pat Duffy, the co-founder of The Giving Block, at a conference. He and his co-founder Alex Wilson had created a best-in-class, turnkey platform to help nonprofits accept approved cryptocurrencies and immediately sell them. The quick turnaround eliminated the risk related to the volatility of cryptocurrencies. The Giving Block also created viral campaigns to help nonprofits engage crypto communities. At the time, they advised only a handful of nonprofit clients. With fledgling media buzz around the growth of crypto, people who wanted to invest in nonprofits via cryptocurrency presented a mostly-untapped potential.

"Nonprofits need to honor the idea of virtuous profit when talking with potential investors, and corporations can benefit from focusing more on opportunities than pity."

Dick Greenly Board Chair, Water4

Renewed testing started with expert guidance. All was going well until we were hit by a bad actor who attempted to donate ill-gotten money to CI. Thankfully, we caught and rejected the transaction. CI cooperated fully with investigators. This experience and the media coverage of it shook our faith and prompted CI to step back. Like many companies and nonprofits, CI is wary of negative media coverage that could tarnish its brand and impede future engagement of partners and donors. They feared this would bleed over into traditional markets, so they adopted a cautious approach, implementing a six-month halt to accepting cryptocurrencies and pausing all relationships within crypto communities.

This wise decision was followed by something fascinating. The social media coverage spawned a wave of sympathy in crypto communities for Children International. All of a sudden, CI went from being unknown in these communities to enjoying a positive spotlight. Out of a scary controversy came something quite good. Leaders in the Elongate community, a relatively young crypto community, reached out to CI to explore how they might help. The leadership in this community was impressed by the pristine record of CI operations, its global reach, and its concrete impact on lifting children out of poverty. CI learned about the community's needs, too. Elongate wanted to channel funds to a good cause, focusing on the natural advocacy of their members, and boosting positive perceptions of their community as good global citizens. Additionally, they wanted a partner that would be an active part of their community. The conversation was much broader than checks and halos.

The communication with Elongate eased CI's fears, and we agreed to a test. CI's CEO joined a live conversation with the larger Elongate community, and CI staff supported the event with messaging through normal social media channels. In a few short months, the relationship with Elongate generated over $400,000 in unrestricted revenue while helping position the Elongate community as a group with heart. The success built confidence for working in this new channel for both partners.

Another important factor in being able to push norms in an organization is how accurate information is delivered succinctly by trusted experts. The wrong person sharing incomplete messages with critical stakeholders can undermine opportunities. Have you ever left a proposal on the CEO's desk just to find out that her administrative staff read it and verbally summarized it incompletely? Bosses are busy and rely on smart staff to help them move fast. When gatekeepers or other influencers understand only parts of a complex opportunity, however, the incomplete pictures they paint can be costly. Those that hear them, especially if they speak with conviction, can mistakenly believe they know enough to form solid opinions. Once those positions are firm, changing them can be difficult.

Here's a story that relates the importance of the right messenger and good information. The American Cancer Society had to inform its board on key public messaging. The board didn't officially have veto power over public relations campaigns, but they could halt something in its tracks if they felt strongly enough. At the time, ACS board members were largely older, white men who were expert medical types. Few had marketing or advertising backgrounds. The day's discussion focused on anti-smoking ads targeting young girls, developed through research. The data indicated that the ads could successfully influence girls to resist smoking.

After the research presentation, ACS's advertising agency shared the spot with the board. The members didn't seem too attentive during the research segment, but the ad got everyone to sit up straight. It was edgy, featuring a beautiful female model smoking and striding down a fashion runway. As she twirled, a tar-like substance began to stick to her. She began to look hideous. She stopped twirling and screamed. The tagline: "If what happens on the inside happened on the outside, would you smoke?" Obviously, this wasn't targeting older, male doctors. In hindsight, maybe we should have briefed one of the influential doctors in advance and had him open the presentation. His stamp of approval and emphasis that the ad was intended for young girls, not older doctors, might have resulted in a less animated and shorter board discussion. The board represented some of the best minds in the world regarding medical research, but they knew little about marketing or what drives teenage behavior. Fortunately, they endorsed the campaign.

Another example of pushing norms deals with the gaming industry, a popular arena that ACS's sports marketing VP recognized for its partnership potential. Atlanta is ACS's headquarters and the city is also a worldwide hub for gaming. The League of Legends championship audience exceeds that of the Super Bowl over streaming (non-traditional TV) platforms. Traditional sponsors like Honda, Allstate, and Mastercard all underwrite these events. Several of these same companies were ACS sponsors, and they wanted ACS to join them in the gaming world. The companies felt that adding a philanthropic element to gaming could benefit gamers, ACS, and its sponsors. Passing on this offer was a missed opportunity and remains so.

The final example of pushing norms involves the Ultimate Fighting Championship and the American Cancer Society. Again, creating partnerships in new arenas is not for the faint of heart. Picking the wrong group to work with can be costly. Ill-fitting partners can create backlash from key constituents and diminish an entity's public perception. This story focuses on brand alignment. A company or nonprofit's brand persona—the type of energy a brand emits—also needs to be a fit in the eyes of stakeholders. For example, the energy drink Redbull has the persona of a courageous, risk-taking, high-energy experience, and it wouldn't work well in a tie-in with a meditative, spa experience.

The American Cancer Society's brand expression has relied heavily on "combat language" since its inception. Phrasing like "fighting cancer" has been popular, and their logo incorporates what most see simply as a sword. It is the image of the caduceus (a sword with two snakes often used as a symbol of medicine). Advocacy groups connected to the cancer cause used labels like the "Women's Field Army" or "Arnie's Army" to reinforce the spirit of the "war on cancer." Logically, you might think that a partner with a focus on fighting might be a fit for ACS, but there was little internal appetite for it.

The Ultimate Fighting Championship (UFC) is focused on mixed martial arts fighting. Its roots are from ancient Greece, and although it started in the US, it is a global, multibillion dollar phenomena. UFC has a huge following. Many of the fighters are superstars with a massive fan base. They are also known to be quite generous. The fight events make huge money, and although fighters abide by rules, the brutality of the events is inescapable.

Even though the ACS frequently uses combat language to demonize the foe of cancer, the ACS leadership felt queasy about the optics of aligning with a violent fight event. Leadership couldn't see past the imagery of UFC to entertain any exploration of partnering. We'll never know if ACS might have been able to generate an appropriate fit since they chose not to push this boundary.

Reflections

What new trends could open doors to new partnerships for you?

What new business categories might be opportunities for you?

What internal discussion needs to occur to foster testing and learning around new trends?

LEVERAGE THE POWER IN PROCESS

Given all the internal complexities I've laid out, it makes sense to be strategic about internal processes and alliances. If you are fortunate, you can build processes from scratch based on best practices and adjust them for the unique realities facing your organization. One of the nice things about starting from scratch is not having to dance around existing structures and emotional attachments to status quo operations. That said, a blank slate has its challenges, too. Start-ups require time to work out software bugs, negotiate support systems, and find the right team. Some organizations don't have the patience for the build-out and want to see results quickly. Whatever your situation, I recommend you engage an outside expert to conduct an audit of the systems, processes, and structures currently in place. Outside voices can help you advocate for needed changes and budget. This is especially true if the change involves multiple departments with attachments to old ways of doing business.

Here are some key underpinnings to creating ideal internal processes and systems:

BUILD INTERNAL PARTNERSHIPS

Secure top leadership support for necessary investments and authority. Whether you are in start-up mode or working with a mature operation, secure the resources and authority necessary to conduct partnership business. Build a case for what you need that includes triggers for additional investment as the ROI builds over time.

Make and keep friends. Get to know and stay in touch with your primary internal stakeholders (legal, finance, PR/communications, program staff, local decision-makers/influencers). Make sure you understand what they need to succeed in their roles. Connect their needs to your mutual success—Help them do well and look good whenever you can. When I start at new jobs, I begin with what I call listening tours. I want to know what everyone thinks and hear about any roadblocks they see to growing partnerships.

Understand what you have in place and what needs to be built. Don't mess with what already works well. Applaud them, build on them, and enlist those doing well in the plan to strengthen weaknesses. Then, build what doesn't exist. At Children International, our biggest asset was a senior team that believed in investing in infrastructure to support partnership building. Another asset was a phenomenal team of researchers who helped us build out prospect research and enhance the usage of our CRM. We found that we also needed to rebuild in-country and program staff knowledge and support of partnerships.

Be a good internal customer. Be clear about your needs and timelines. Be flexible when you can and easy to work with. Avoid surprises. Don't take co-workers for granted. Remember: "Your urgency isn't my emergency." Make sure they know that any last- minute requests were not rooted in lack of planning.

Make accountability agreements with everyone. Those who play a role in partnership building must also be accountable for that role and the necessary deliverables. One weak link can damage partner relationships.

Offer incentives. Make it worth their while to prioritize your needs. Support is strongest when you can reward a person for their support. If you understand their needs, pain points, and concerns, you can often help them, and that help is essentially an incentive.

Celebrate together and share the glory. When you win big, make sure everyone feels the glow of success and can take pride in their involvement. After all, you couldn't have done it without everyone playing their parts.

The key systems and processes you need to support partnership-building include:

CRM system. Having a good one tailored to your needs and goals can't be emphasized enough. The platform must be easy for reps to use and geared to display progress against all individual and team success indicators. Reps and team leaders need to be incentivized to live in this system as they plan, track, and strategize. It also needs to be able to map relationships and tie related accounts together.

Key Performance Indicators (KPIs). All of the important deliverables necessary for a highly functioning core partnership team and support teams need to be spelled out, assigned, and measured. What is measured is more likely to become a clear priority. KPIs allow you to see potential fail points quickly and to celebrate the necessary underpinnings involved in building and sustaining partnerships.

Financial reporting. Although partnership building involves many measurable impacts, it always involves finances. Money is king and can drive the organizational value seen in partnerships. In the nonprofit world, when reporting to the Board of Directors, revenue from partnerships is often incorporated in the finance department's overall financial reporting. I find it preferable that partnership revenue data come directly from the CRM system. Having to force fit data between CRM software and financial software systems can be a frustrating time suck.

Research. You need many kinds of research for an optimal partnership operation as well as the time to translate the data into plans and course corrections. The research list includes account movement, prospect modeling and identification, messaging, trends, competitive data, and much more.

Internal stakeholders check-ins and reports. The right processes can help you stay close to your internal stakeholders and cultivate their support. Use check-ins to spot potential problems early and to prevent emergencies. These check-ins also provide an opportunity to highlight their unique contributions and to celebrate accomplishments.

Leadership engagement. Having a system in place to showcase leadership support will make the work of partnerships easier and more productive. By including regular reports in leadership meetings, you can harness the power of leadership regarding your budget, goals, and involvement in partner engagement.

Incentives. Beyond the KPIs mentioned earlier, if you can formalize individual and team incentives through monetary and nonmonetary rewards, you'll achieve greater results. Be sure to include key contributors from other departments as well as local and regional staff.

Celebration. Make this more than part of a staff meeting or a check-in. Build celebration and the intent to learn from each other's wins and losses in all gatherings of the people who make the partnerships work. Make it a strong thread in your organizational culture, and it will yield results.

That is a pretty good list, but when you think about systems and processes, challenge yourself to think beyond best practices and normal checklists. Consider any unique circumstances or stumbling blocks you may be facing. Can you create a system or process tailored specifically to your situation? When I worked with the American Cancer Society, we faced multiple layers of approval for individual deals. Almost anyone could cast doubt or nix a deal for an array of reasons. The considerations were valuable, but the process for dealing with them was painful, so we applied a unique remedy. The partner criteria covered in Chapter Two was developed by working with a board committee. Board level buy-in equated to permission to pursue any corporate relationship that met the majority of those criteria. Essentially, this equated to pre-approval at the highest level. We incorporated accountability checks, including quarterly reports to the board, on all new partnerships. Departmental support for each partnership still needed to be negotiated, but the criteria and regular board involvement minimized issues in advance, allowing us to move more quickly in building deals. Board reports also offered an opportunity to praise other departments or diplomatically identify difficulties. This example demonstrates how you don't have to live with issues that slow you down. Think creatively about your organization's challenges and employ best practices and expert knowledge, but leave room for unique solutions to special circumstances.

Internal support isn't just needed as you negotiate partnership details. It is also crucial to fulfilling agreements. Once an arrangement is in place, you depend on different internal resources to honor the contract. I remember one animated conversation with the communications department when partnership agreements were getting "bumped" by urgent work for other internal constituents. I felt empathy for the pressure of serving many masters, but we still had to honor our corporate agreements. Instead of escalating the problem to our boss, we devised a unique solution. I agreed to add money in my budget to expand communication resources. Once we could address the communication leader's problem, we were seen as a helpful client and partner.

Processes and systems have to be dynamic. As we learn and work together, additional good processes can help build success and efficiency. At the same time, some processes that are less helpful should be retired. An example of adding a process to address the needs of an internal group comes from the previously described ACS's work with the Florida Department of Citrus (FDOC). Although program staff in local markets understood the benefit of the advertising campaign that was a big element of the partnership, they didn't have the time to fulfill a promise we made on their behalf: to staff customer information stations at grocery stores. They also didn't see this as the best use of their time or their volunteers' time. This conflict was harder to solve and required us to create an additional criterion for future national partnerships. Going forward, our contracts would not promise local action without approval from local program staff. We created a process to make sure we were all on the same page in the future.

Local staff reaction to the FDOC partnership is understandable. The power they had to stand their ground came from operating in a federated governance model. In this model, decision-making is distributed. Headquarters staff can't simply dictate decisions to chapters or regional staff. I worked under this structure at the American Cancer Society and World Vision. It meant that, even though I represented global headquarters, I could not obligate the affiliates to do anything. Federated governance models require a process for local operations buy-in that bring them into negotiations early and include them as partnerships evolve. This is a point companies need to be aware of when trying to partner with such an organization on a global level.

Processes around regional and local autonomy are also a reality for many global companies which is a fact nonprofits need to keep in mind. For example, when I approached various manufacturers of mammography equipment to explore their investment in the Million Woman Breast Cancer Screening project in China, I was always referred to their China regional offices.

This next story is also an example of building partnerships that respect local and global considerations. The 2017 partnership between Special Olympics (SO) and ESPN/ABC required a sensitive translation of the company's expectations of value (ROI) and their desire for active support from internal stakeholders at Special Olympics. The nonprofit's local staff and volunteers' perception of the value they offered was much higher than the perception of the nonprofit's headquarters staff and that of ESPN/ABC. The negotiation was further complicated by the fact that local chapters had local sponsorship promises that had to meld—not compete or cannibalize—with the activation plans for global relationships.

ESPN/ABC's normal process in partner discussions is to analyze audience ratings to forecast the ultimate value of a concept to their business. Ratings correlated directly to their ability to sell advertising and, therefore, their bottom line. This tangible, non-emotional tool helped adjust local SO chapters' understanding of value and led to a fair investment. The partnership made ESPN/ABC folks feel good, but more importantly, the business proposition required a measurable business win.

This knowledge was empowering to SO. Once they understood what was important to the company, the local and global staff at SO got creative. SO couldn't buy advertising themselves or guarantee a television ratings boost, but they could encourage their other sponsors to advertise, which brought more value to ESPN/ABC. The shifted value equation enabled SO to negotiate a share of revenue from the additional advertising for Special Olympics. ESPN/ABC also added funding from their philanthropic budget. This smart negotiating stemmed from SO's local and global staff working together. In the end, the Special Olympics received $1 million per year. They didn't earn a share of advertising revenue because the final totals weren't high enough to trigger it. The deal did generate more coverage for Special Olympics, though, and the local SO chapter received part of the philanthropic grant dollars.

Reflections

When have processes and systems helped you run your partnership business better?

What processes and systems could be improved to help you run your business better or address a unique situation you are facing?

What internal support do you need to evolve systems and processes?

USE EXPERTS TO CHASE POSSIBILITIES VERSUS LIMITATIONS

Companies come in all shapes and sizes and rely on a variety of revenue models. Likewise, nonprofits are not one size fits all. Charity Navigator, a well-respected oversight entity for the nonprofit space, reworked their evaluation criteria a few years ago when they became painfully aware that one set applied to all nonprofits could not possibly be fair. Whether you represent the corporation or nonprofit, consult with outside experts to help you understand your prospective partner's business, including its needs, motivations, and limitations.

"You cannot look in a new direction by looking harder in the same direction."

Edward de Bono author of *Six Thinking Hats*

When the American Cancer Society explored working with Citibank, we had a CFO with deep corporate financial expertise. Still, we took the extra step of involving volunteers from the banking and credit space to help us understand the specifics of this industry. Beyond knowledge of specific business sectors, using outside experts can be helpful if you are exploring partnership around a variety of business strategies, like entering new markets or launching new products or services. As mentioned earlier, I wish I had retained subject matter experts in retail before the ACS meeting with Walmart.

In addition to subject matter experts, keep an eye on trends to stay ahead of the business curves that they predict. The first to capitalize on what is coming is often the biggest winner. This applies to partnerships, too. One way to stay ahead in this competitive field is to look beyond the current landscape and to imagine opportunities in emerging spaces.

We've already discussed the (then) new frontiers of cryptocurrency and gaming. Operating as an explorer can feel risky, but outside expertise and a willingness to learn by testing can produce powerful partnerships more safely without the competitive pressures found in traditional markets. As previously mentioned, when Children International first entered the cryptocurrency world, they did so with guidance and systems provided by The Giving Block. CI was one of about a dozen nonprofits testing in these early times, and they had success. Within two years, however, the number of nonprofit clients of this one consultancy had jumped to over a thousand. Success attracts the masses!

Companies and nonprofits are busy, and no matter how big they are, they struggle with limited budgets. They must often focus their resources on key business outcomes of any given quarter, leaving little time to stay abreast of trends. These are all great excuses for letting someone else eat your lunch.

Even a sophisticated research department generally has its hands full with tracking data related to the business at hand. When this is the case, rely on third-party trend data and futurists' musings. This is easier if you have an advisory group tracking trends and helping you interpret them. Atlanta's Marketing Roundtable, created by Ken Bernhardt of Georgia State University fame, is a group of senior corporate and nonprofit marketers from non-competitive spaces who gather monthly to discuss trends. Such groups provide a glimpse of what is around the corner when you are too busy to look. Expert advisors can also help you build cases for testing into the future before trends become old news.

Reflections

When could you have used an outside expert? How would that have changed your proposition or informed your negotiations? What practical testing opportunities have outside experts helped you identify relevant and developing trends?

SHARE THE GLORY

We have talked about the power of testing to inform partnership conversations. This section digs a bit deeper and relates testing to how you build internal cohesion and pride through testing. Testing can also often provide data to celebrate all who help generate success.

The American Cancer Society research described earlier with Citibank is a great example. Proving ACS value led to a huge investment from the bank. The win allowed us to also shine a light on the finance department and the CFO as some of the heroes in that story. In another example, ACS's relationship with General Mills resulted from regional market tests. The ability to associate with a cereal product was only possible by the work from the ACS scientific team. The science team assessed which brands were healthy enough for ACS's *de facto* endorsement. We were able to applaud that team as we moved forward with this relationship. Testing provides evidence of value, which is just as important to internal audiences as it is to external audiences. Test results can transform stakeholders from passive observers to active advocates internally. This can be priceless.

Here is a story about the power of testing to influence internal audiences. When I was with the American Cancer Society, the brand was well known publicly and well respected. However, other than medical research related to cancer, most people didn't know what the organization really did. ACS had launched over a hundred independent brands of programs and services. Some of the most well-known were Coaches vs. Cancer, Look Good Feel Better, Patient Navigator, and Relay for Life. These programs had impressive name recognition independent of each other and ACS, and people loved them. Unfortunately, that love didn't translate to monetary support for the programs because the public failed to realize that they were funded through the ACS. We needed to connect to the passion and support generated by our programs, but we encountered internal resistance.

Research to the rescue. Focus group research highlighted the risks of the public disconnect between ACS and its programs in a moving way. In one session, a respondent who had lost his wife to cancer said that he knew of the ACS, but the organization did nothing for his wife when she was fighting for her life. He shared this with a degree of bitterness. Asked what organization had helped during his wife's battle, he replied that *Reach to Recovery* had given his wife hope. His whole body language softened as he detailed the difference this program had made for them and how it deserved support. He had no idea that *Reach to Recovery* was owned and funded by ACS. Neither the program logo nor its materials mentioned ACS in any significant way. This research—namely this story—compelled ACS's leadership and the many program leaders to support a change in brand architecture for ACS and all its programs.

With that broad support, ACS retired over 100 independent logos and developed a standard visual to connect ACS program names to the master brand name and logo. Over time, the ACS made progress in building public understanding that a donation to ACS funded the programs and services they valued. Without research and testing, we would have struggled to convince internal staff or volunteers to accept this important change.

Research and the appropriate dialogue around findings can help address all kinds of issues related to developing partnerships. Remember that when The Coca-Cola Company and World Wildlife Fund first started talking, neither side below the top leadership felt that they could find common ground. Thankfully, that changed. Even then, they couldn't begin rolling out programs together without research. They had to test, learn, and prove value internally for both organizations. This negotiation became a success story, and most Americans see a beloved match between Coke and pandas now.

One other note on the value of testing: If you have any doubt that you—or your prospective partner—can deliver what you hope for, begin testing. Don't offer anything you are not certain you cannot provide. Failing to deliver in a partnership sours not only the specific partnership, but can also taint your reputation and poison future conversations. The partnership world is a small one, and word definitely gets around. This is also a relevant point regarding internal stakeholders. Staff stay engaged when they feel good about wins. Failure looks bad on everyone and dampens enthusiasm for future involvement in partnerships.

Finally, I believe that testing is good stewardship for companies and nonprofits. The information from research findings can create efficiencies in decision-making and can be a point of pride for boards, leadership staff, and all who touch partnerships. Achieving fair value for the ACS-Citibank deal bolstered everyone internally to continue to pursue similar relationships. It also helped me win a budget to fund market testing for future opportunities.

Reflections

When would data have helped you negotiate for internal support in a better way? What kinds of data could you have used?

When has data helped you negotiate?

What do you find hard to prove when assessing the value of a program or service? Think about this again from the perspective of the prospective partner? What new ideas come to mind when considering value from their perspective?

How have you used testing to celebrate internal partners? How did this impact your internal relationships?

ALWAYS CONSIDER TIMING

The economy, markets, technology, demand for services and products: all are in constant flux. What is relevant to people and organizations changes rapidly. Partnerships that are good ideas today may become even better over time. They could also become stale. Keep track of external changes because they can disrupt partnerships if you don't pivot with the flow of change.

Internal changes can create disruption or opportunity as well. These can include staff turnover, changes in strategy, restructuring of organizational leadership or power, and more. Remember that everything has a season and a time. To stay relevant in a relationship, stay alert to changes so you can pivot and sharpen how you bring value with respect to evolving realities.

TOMS shoes found lightning in a bottle with their "buy one, give one" shoe offer. Celebrities loved the idea, and business took off. TOMS brokered partnerships with various nonprofit organizations focused on alleviating poverty. Children International fit their strategy, and the partnership enabled TOMS to distribute thousands of shoes to children in need while providing employee engagement opportunities and powerful stories for the company and CI to share with constituents.

Over time, the model was replicated by other retail companies and no longer differentiated TOMS. The idea had run its course, forcing the company to pivot. TOMS developed a new strategy to reinvigorate customer enthusiasm. Unfortunately for CI, the new strategy focused on current issues in select US markets, areas that were not relevant for CI. The partnership had been successful, but its time had passed.

The fluidity of connections in organizations can also create timing issues. People come and go. You may have a wonderful relationship in a company or a nonprofit, but having only one can make you vulnerable. When that person moves on, you are caught in limbo with no one to turn to. Often, a new person will want to distinguish themselves by moving in a different direction with strategy, and your partnership may be deemed irrelevant. Double whammy! No individual relationship and no relevance. To protect your organization against such situations, aim to cultivate multiple contacts within a partner organization. Jane Turner did a great job of this in the story I shared about the Atlanta Children's Museum.

The space most known for volatility and change is social media, and this can be a source of huge disruption—or a huge opportunity. It all depends on timing and your ability to quickly navigate change. Think back to the cryptocurrency stories. Social media time and digital communities move fast. Circumstances change quickly. You have to remain nimble to take advantage of opportunities in this space.

Another interesting arena where timing can be everything involves earned media opportunities. These windows of opportunity often follow news cycles that rise and disappear in a matter of days. Environmental crises break and are supplanted by other events in short order. Disaster relief organizations must be poised to act within hours to secure funders for targeted help. Delays may result in companies donating to other entities or focusing on a "fresher" need. One of my team members at World Vision was a master at reaching out to companies quickly in times of disaster. He used a template of common disaster needs and costs and maintained a list of companies with a demonstrated affinity for disaster relief efforts. He could produce proposals and generate funds within hours of a crisis.

Controversy can present a time-based opportunity, too. In 2021, Vice President Kamala Harris flew to Central America to discuss the underlying causes of mass immigration which put the plight of children at the U.S. border into sharper focus. For a time, the media was all over her visit, looking for different angles to report. At that time, nonprofits that had proven solutions to root causes could have engaged in the conversation in a powerful way and on a national level. Of course, the political polarization of the time meant risk, but the window of opportunity was unquestionable. Executed wisely, the participation of experts from respected nonprofits in this controversy could have had a far-reaching impact on children and families at that moment. I recommended that one organization in particular step into the conversation, but they saw the risk of potentially offending supporters as too high.

Prepare yourself to consider opportunities in the face of crisis and controversy. A timely and measured response can help you realize benefits for your organization including higher visibility and garnering the interest of new customers or investors.

Reflections

When have you been in the right place at just the right time to initiate a partner conversation?

How nimble is your organization to take advantage of time-sensitive opportunities?

What organizations do you feel are particularly responsive?

How might your organization be better prepared to respond to fast-moving situations?

STOKE LOCAL POWER AND PRIDE

—

Let's shift gears. Please keep in mind that this section is not intended to beat up on corporate or nonprofit headquarters staff. If you made the grade to work at headquarters, you are smart and have plenty to offer the bottom line, whether it is measured in dollars or mission. This section is about remembering the power of local intelligence and experience. Everyone wins when we tap those assets. A great story about the power and impact of partnership between global, regional, and local staff involves Marriott and Women for Women International (WfWI). The conviction and passion of local staff from both entities created a mutual win with ripple effects around the world.

When Marriott built a new hotel in Kigali, Rwanda, they wanted to show appreciation for the warm welcome of local businesses, community leaders, and government. They also believed that a vibrant local economy was directly related to the health of their business. Plus, investing specifically in growing a local workforce with hospitality skill sets enabled them to address their future needs with good works. One of the organizations they chose to help address their ongoing need for trained hospitality employees was Women for Women International.

WfWI offers women who have been the victims of war a chance to heal and build better futures for themselves and their children. Many of the women have experienced horrific violence and have been shunned by their own communities because they are no longer seen as desirable. The nonprofit enrolls these women in training programs that teach them work skills and how to run micro businesses. Their success rate is impressive. More than 80,000 women have been touched by this program since its inception in 1997. Once these women are successful economically, they are often accepted back into their communities. Some have even employed others and contributed to a greater community well-being.

Marriott did more than throw money at this program to secure a local halo. To demonstrate their commitment to building a strong community, they offered WfWI hospitality employment positions for the women enrolled in their program. This required that the women participate in a competitive hiring process. The positions were reserved for them if they could demonstrate high-level proficiency in hospitality tasks.

The offer was exciting, but the fit was initially problematic. One of the biggest issues was that the WfWI women had never set foot in a hotel. Many didn't sleep on mattresses and were not familiar with the art of making beds. Most of them didn't have electricity or running water in their homes. In short, they were totally unfamiliar with the hotel environment and lacked experience in using a vacuum, making a bed, or cleaning bathrooms.

Fortunately, local Marriott and WfWI staff didn't back away from each other. They talked about the challenge and devised a plan. Marriott's HR leadership offered a training class to instruct the WfWI job candidates on the hotel's cleaning protocols. The trainees would then have 15 minutes to clean a room by themselves. If they passed this skills test, they would be given a position alongside employees from more privileged backgrounds. Everyone thought this was a creative and fair approach. Well, hold that thought. They hadn't asked the women in the WfWI program about it yet.

This wasn't easy to sell to local women living in poverty. WfWI staff decided that the best way to serve up this opportunity was to approach someone who was seen as an influencer in their participant group. They chose a middle-aged woman who lived a walkable distance from the new hotel. They hoped that if she were interested, others would follow her lead. I met this warm, kind, and funny woman during a visit to the Marriott's Rwanda facility a few years later. I wanted to witness the program in action and to hear from the participants themselves about how the work changed their lives.

The woman told me that her first meeting with WfWI staff was a bit rocky. She told her story with a mixture of humor and humility. Essentially, she politely but flatly declined the offer to interview for work at any hotel. She delivered her answer with a good dose of indignation to boot. Understandably, the staff felt deflated and puzzled. They didn't want to leave the woman feeling irritable, so they kept the conversation going, and, in doing so, began to understand why she felt the way she did. They learned that the only women she knew who worked at hotels were prostitutes. This woman of high moral standards was in no way interested in that line of work! Everyone was quite relieved when she and the other women understood that *that* was not the employment being offered.

With the misunderstanding resolved, the woman's next question was whether she would have to wear the short dresses and low-cut blouses like those she had seen maids wear in magazines. She felt too old for that type of uniform. This, too, was clarified to her satisfaction, but the questions and assumptions were just a foretaste of the challenge of working in a place so vastly different than anything she'd ever experienced before. She did end up competing and winning a position at the hotel. Her stories about running a vacuum and an electric sewing machine for the first time are true belly laugh stories. Most who trained did win jobs, and they all worked hard.

There is more to the story. The women from more affluent parts of town looked down on the women from the poorer neighborhoods. They didn't want to work with women whom they felt were beneath them. It got so bad that the women from privilege threatened to quit if Marriott didn't fire the "others." Thankfully, hotel management shared some information that quelled the unrest. One of the key performance indicators for housekeeping staff was feedback from hotel customers. This feedback showed that the women from impoverished areas were the most helpful, responsive, and courteous of all employees. The management refused to release the very employees who were winning the most adulation from its customers.

Another heartwarming part of this partnership was the impact on the day-to-day lives of the program's participants. One of the women shared how she was treated by shopkeepers prior to her employment at Marriott and how this changed after she started working. Because she had no money, she wasn't welcome in the shops. If she did enter, she was watched closely because shopkeepers feared she might steal. She didn't hold her head high when walking by public places. She tried to shrink into the background because she didn't feel she had a right to even be there. This all changed when she took the hotel job. She was invited into stores and even offered credit. She walked confidently now with a feeling of value and belonging.

This story highlights the ripple effect of success when a company's business goals for a local partnership tie well with a nonprofit. It further demonstrates how honoring local perspectives and experience when developing the relationship makes all the difference. Any success without such local involvement will likely be anemic compared to achievements with local buy-in. A good-sized check for a charity and a bit of ROI for a company alone is not enough to generate astounding success. You have to impact lives. This is the strongest measure of good corporate citizenship. Headquarters staff have a huge role to play, but they can't fully grasp the reality and nuances from afar. Success stories like this make all staff prouder and more invested in their work.

Let's talk about that last sentence just a bit more. We must understand the intended and unintended consequences of a partnership to the customer as well as to the beneficiaries. Lean on local knowledge to find magical stories and make sure they know that they played a role in creating the goodness in those stories. After all, without customers, Marriott could not succeed, much less do so in a way that created more good in the world. This not only makes the partnership a win from their perspective, but allows you to amplify real-life stories that can resonate throughout both partner organizations.

Reflections

Do you actively seek perspectives from local markets? How has this impacted your partnerships?

When might an initiative have turned out differently had you sought local feedback?

Chapter 5

PLACE TRUST AT THE CENTER

Relationships grow when trust blooms between parties. Without trust, not much will come from even the finest glitter and words. That said, you can't sprinkle trust dust and magically turn things around either. Developing this foundation takes time, maybe even a couple of years from the start of partner conversations to the execution of a contract. Pro-tip for nonprofits: Never take a job where they want you to take partnerships from zero to millions in one fiscal year. Partnership building requires time, resources, and patience because the relationship rides on mutual respect and faith in each other.

Establishing this foundation relies on consistent actions more than words. The wrong action can jeopardize the relationship lightning quick. Failing to deliver what you promise

159

or missing a deadline will weaken a partner's faith. Knowing about problems early on and failing to confer with your partner will also damage the relationship.

Building trust grows more complicated with multiple cooks in the kitchen. Although more challenging with more people involved, complex relationships are a bit like a rope in that it is stronger with more threads as long as the threads are well entwined. The more people working on an account, the greater the opportunity for broad affinity, but keeping actions and messaging consistent can also be more difficult.

At World Vision, the development team negotiated partner and donor opportunities, but a different department, the program team, usually fulfilled them. When sales and fulfillment weren't on the same page, partners felt it. I remember my team being at odds with program staff who were months behind on building wells. They had good reasons but didn't communicate them in a timely manner, which made it difficult to manage the company's expectations. Regrettably, we had to return funds because we couldn't fulfill our contractual obligations. Failure to do what we said we'd do and failure to divulge the problems in advance broke the partner's faith. Securing funding from that company again was an uphill battle. The pain wasn't limited to that relationship alone. As was said before, the partnership world is small enough that problems with one company can easily jeopardize conversations with others.

The most important keys to building trust are:

• Clearly communicate in a timely manner
• Keep promises

- Avoid unpleasant surprises
- Keep your partner's interests in mind

With these keys engaged, you'll see relationships grow as well as another interesting dynamic. New ideas can emerge from the fertile ground that might be totally unrelated to the existing agreement. These may spur spontaneous opportunities to grow together. Such thinking can bring more mutual value such as suggestions for pivots ahead of potential issues or ways to expand the involvement of other partners.

"Authenticity is key to trusted and long-lasting relationships."

Damon Taugher former VP Global Programs for Direct Relief

All that said, I have found one shortcut to building trust. I call it secondhand trust. This is when a person has faith in you simply because someone they already love and respect tells them they can depend on you. That's magical. It is one of the highest honors in partnership building. This phenomena arises from reputations developed over time. Literally, your reputation precedes you. Secondhand trust is a precious gift, and it deserves a story.

I was introduced by email to a new potential partner by someone I had worked with for several years. I offered to bring the new person on a trip to see our work and to give him a chance to acquaint himself with me and the organization. He declined, saying, "If Dave trusts you, I trust you." We likely skipped a year of courtship and moved straight to exploring a partnership.

Whether a relationship unfolds slowly or quickly, be sure to match the depth of the trust you have established with the risk level for your partner concepts. Higher levels of complexity and risk require deeper levels of trust. Confidence must run deep enough to carry the weight of the invitation you wish to extend. Small requests with little risk don't require as much faith as complex and risky requests. If you jump ahead before establishing an adequate foundation, you will likely encounter rejection or delays. Delay tactics take all kinds of forms: requests for additional information or evidence to support the concept, requests for other noted experts to weigh in, and even requests for other departmental opinions, including finance and legal. These can be legitimate due diligence intended to boost comfort levels or they can be devious ways to bury a scary idea. Here's a kicker: if they have to go to all that effort to avoid risk, doing so will also tarnish you in their eyes. Bringing a partner something that uncomfortable can lead them to doubt your expertise or question that you have their best interest in mind. Moving too fast without the appropriate level of trust can stymie progress and potentially damage your reputation.

Reflections

When has trust been challenged in a partnership that you or someone else was managing? What caused the breakdown? How have you repaired situations where trust has been damaged?

LISTEN AND AVOID ASSUMPTIONS

—

Making assumptions can seriously undermine relationships. Some presumptions are right on the mark, and, expressed thoughtfully, they can save you time and energy. Assumptions that are off base, however, are the ones that can prevent you from tuning in to what is important. These can potentially slam the door on opportunities. This point warrants an exclamation point! Poor assumptions can send a partner conversation into a death spiral. Remain mindful of your preconceptions and check them before launching negotiations.

Dangerous Assumptions:

You know what the other person is going to say before they say it. Here are two possible results of believing this. First, you might lose the opportunity to learn something new and potentially important to building the relationship. If you find yourself thinking about what you are going to say rather than listening, you are likely operating under this assumption and missing what's being said. Second, assuming you know what will be said makes you come off as tone deaf and self-centered. These aren't likable or trustworthy traits. Generally speaking, likable people are more trusted and secure more partnerships.

You already know the main reason the other person is at the table. Maybe you do, but double-check. Maybe they have a genuine interest in your idea, or maybe they are simply being polite. Maybe a friend or a higher-up told them they had to meet with you. If you assume incorrectly, you have crossed wires before you start talking. When I met the brand manager at General Mills, I knew he was only there because a mutual friend asked him to give me a meeting. Knowing this, I was prepared to quickly demonstrate relevance to his top issues: price and profit. If I had assumed interest in my cause and talked about that, I would have gotten the polite boot after my allotted 15 minutes.

You believe the other party read the materials you sent ahead of time. Arriving at meetings fully prepared is ideal, but people are busy. You can't assume they had time to learn about you, your organization, or your ideas. The sad part is that they'll get bored if you rattle on about yourself and your organization during the meeting. You'll also irritate the handful of those who actually read the materials you sent. The rule of top three can help:

1. Relay succinctly the top three things about you and your organization that are most relevant to the partner and the opportunity at hand. These differentiate you from others and quickly communicate your relevance.
2. List the three most powerful benefits of your proposal.
3. Listen more than you talk. Answer questions, ask for clarifications, and wrap up by specifying next steps.

Your prospective partner has your best interests in mind. This is going to sound a bit jaded, but stay with me. Most people are courteous in meetings, but that doesn't mean they like you, your organization, or your idea. We would love it if everyone came to meetings with a win/win mindset, but people often have other priorities on their minds: deadlines, performance reviews, and personal life challenges. If you assume someone has your best interests in mind, you may also misread their behavior. In China, people were exceedingly nice to me. They would smile, nod, and feed me to no end, but that didn't equal support for me or my proposals. There, anything less than a resounding yes is a polite no. If you are prone to this assumption, be sure to listen deeply and to ask questions about possible obstacles while reinforcing benefits. Being politely candid can also help you navigate past the social niceties.

You are a top priority for your prospective partner. Even if this is true, they have other priorities vying for their attention. Blind to this, you can come off as somewhat naive or narcissistic. Confidence in yourself is a great trait as long as it doesn't devolve into arrogance. The latter doesn't build trust and can actually obstruct moving conversations forward. Some organizations employ creative attention-grabbing tactics. A company once sent me a color TV with a video player so I'd watch their introduction tape and grant them a meeting. It worked. I took the meeting, but I returned the equipment afterward, of course.

You believe that companies and nonprofits have inherent character flaws or some sort of self-serving intention. A common negative assumption about companies is that they are solely seeking their own gain and may exploit partners. Corporations may assume that nonprofits aren't business-minded and just want money. These assumptions do not serve anyone well. If a company or nonprofit really has fatal flaws according to your sense of ethics, discover them early and move on to other partners that promise a better alignment.

Your idea of success is your partner's idea of success. Remember the

Boys and Girls Clubs of America story about their partnership with a bank? Staff were proud of the stats on employee morale and media coverage. Unfortunately, the bank's measure of success was increased credit card usage. If you want longevity in a partnership, fully understand everyone's key goals and set concrete measures for all of them.

Time is fluid. Whether you are talking about meeting times or the timeline for key deliverables, time is rarely fluid. You may be granted more time in certain situations, but treat time as a precious commodity and honor deadline-sensitive obligations.

Being bold is bad. You really don't want to spook someone with your biggest, boldest idea on the first date. Make sure you have established a level of trust that gives you permission to be bold. If you've done your homework and believe you have a strong fit, then be bold. Include testing as a pathway to build confidence toward the big payoff.

Interrogate your assumptions. Let your past experience and your own intuition inform them. Remain humble enough, though, to recognize that your assumption may be off base. You can pay a high price by not questioning yourself. Discover what is real by listening attentively to your partner and observing their behavior.

Two more notes on listening. First, nonverbal communication can provide a wealth of information. Furrowed eyebrows, smiles, and crossed arms can cue you to reinforce messages, invite questions or objections, and even pivot if needed. Secondly, work to tune in to what people are saying. We all want to speak eloquently, but too much attention to crafting a verbal response distracts us from what is being said. Consider the risk of not hearing everything accurately or misreading body language. If you aren't paying attention and the other person is being vague or overly diplomatic, you miss even more points and opportunities to ask clarifying questions. This all adds up to a missed opportunity to build relationships by demonstrating attentiveness, empathy, and respect.

By listening carefully, you can reflect your partner's perspectives as you brainstorm ideas. Asking people to help you better understand their point demonstrates that you care. The real cost of poor listening is forfeiting the opportunity to develop a plan that everyone owns and that excites everyone. Most importantly, we miss out on strengthening the foundations of any relationship: trust and respect.

Reflections

When have you realized that an assumption you made in a partnership discussion was off base? How did this impact your conversation and relationship?

What kind of assumptions are you prone to make? How can you prevent your assumptions from undermining you?

DELIVER ON PROMISES AND PREVENT SURPRISES

The old phrase "bait and switch" comes to mind. Faith in relationships will evaporate if you don't do what you say you'll do. You might be able to recover if you have a good reason for the failure and you are sufficiently remorseful about it. Still, try to do what you say and minimize surprises. Even small misses can have a long tail. People remember when you failed them, and this affects their future interactions with you.

This story is about a partnership I worked on with a small tourism company that offered something similar to mission trips for teenagers. The idea was to further the cultural exchange by creating service and sports activities for U.S. teens from middle to upper income families to enjoy with teens living in economically depressed conditions in other countries. The nonprofit was responsible for the in-country experience and all promotional materials. The company provided the U.S. recruitment of teens and coordinated transportation and lodging logistics. The trip was canceled with almost no notice because the company failed to meet its recruitment target. The ROI wasn't there. Unfortunately, the company did not reimburse the nonprofit for its outlay in setting up the local experience. Needless to say, we didn't attempt another pilot with this company.

The earlier story about a nonprofit unable to meet deadlines for drilling wells is also an example of lapse in promises and an unwelcome surprise to a partner. Surprises can come in many forms. I recall one time when a senior officer of a nonprofit met with a significant investor to deliver options for creative partnering. The investor liked the options, but the real driver of interest was his relationship with the senior officer. Shortly after an initial payment on the proposal was made, the senior officer left the organization with no notice to the investor. The relationship was salvaged, but the lack of transparency about known shifts in employment certainly rocked that boat.

Reflections

When have you done an excellent job of fulfilling all obligations of a partnership? How did that impact the relationship and future discussions?

When have you missed deadlines or key outcomes? How did you try to repair the situation? How did this impact the relationship and future discussions?

BUILD BIG TRUST FOR BIG IDEAS

—

Anybody can sell a little idea with few moving parts as long as the value matches the cost. Little ideas aren't bad. They create good in the world that shouldn't be dismissed. Big ideas, on the other hand, can generate exponentially bigger impacts. They require a greater foundation of trust. They can also generate monstrous failures, failures that can obliterate a relationship.

Risk comes with the territory of partnerships. Big ideas involve like-sized risks. You can test, pilot, and plan to reduce those risks, but you never eliminate all of them. People don't take significant risks with shallow trust and respect, but we've talked enough about that. Be clear: the bigger the risk, the deeper the need for faith in your partner. This faith equates to a living connection that can grow or wane. Once you establish this foundation, it is not done. You must consistently demonstrate worthiness. Any actions that weaken the relationship won't weather the complications that inevitably arise in a complex partnership. To advance big idea partnerships, invest in building relationships with a strong foundation of trust and keep feeding confidence in the relationship.

"Only when you partner with those with strategic contributions to a shared vision can you create joint value that is sustainable."

Ramesh Subramaniam former Partner, Consequent, and former Head of Strategy and Marketing, Channels and Alliances, Equifax

---

Remember that this kind of relationship isn't just a key to external parties. High levels of trust within your organization are also critical because risk is usually shared among multiple departments. If a partnership arrangement goes badly, public relations, finance, programs, legal, and other departments will likely feel the fallout, too. They need to believe you are covering all the bases to ensure success and minimize complications. The Coca-Cola and World Wildlife Foundation partnership around sustainable water sources discussed earlier is a great example of building respect both internally and externally with phenomenal success.

Reflections

When have you been able to pull off a bold idea because you had the trust and respect of others involved? How did you gain and maintain those relationships?

When have you seen efforts to do something bold falter because of a lack of trust in partners' ability to execute? This applies to internal and external relationships.

LEARN FROM FAILURE

—

The idea of "covering all the bases" to cultivate a bond of trust is actually a broader concept with a richer end. Think beyond making sure contracts are buttoned up or that the PR team has the bandwidth to activate or that your local team will actually follow through. Think past testing and piloting and measuring outcomes. What happens when we do all that? We contribute to the growth of a very special kind of culture in our organizations.

This is a culture of learning, improving, and celebrating with each other. We move as one rather than a bunch of parts. Good leaders build teams that co-own issues as they arise and collectively celebrate successes. This won't happen without a strong, cross-cutting belief that partnership as a strategy is core to the organization's mission and business success. The resulting bond then exists within the cultural fabric and values of the organization. Executing a partnership deal isn't just about the business outcomes. The people executing the day-to-day work are the ones who impact customer behavior and beneficiaries' lives, so ensure that their "why I'm here" isn't answered with "it's just a job." You don't realize radically successful partnerships with people unless you understand them and demonstrate that you want them to succeed, too. Relationships grounded like this will see greater reliability and commitment from all involved.

This kind of team is more like a fellowship of partnership makers. At this level, people stay in touch even when they move from job to job. They become friends who support each other in personal circumstances. This cohesion can help stabilize partnerships, even those with a tremendous variety of moving parts and personalities. This level of partnership is fed by shared credit when things go phenomenally well, shared ownership when things go off course, and constant learning from the pleasant and the painful. This relationship focus fosters the kind of connection that endures throughout careers, and, in my experience, correlates to the most impactful partnerships.

Reflections

How have you included internal and external partners in celebrating success? How does this celebration impact relationships?

How have you built shared ownership for stumbles? How does this impact the team?

CHOOSE MESSENGERS WISELY

—

The right messenger can build trust. The wrong one can erode it. This can be true when communicating seemingly innocuous information but is most apparent when handling sensitive information. An example of a seemingly mundane blunder is when a partner comes to visit with their senior leadership in tow, and your senior leadership is too busy to welcome them. A welcome message delivered by a junior member of the organization will land differently. This basic nicety can set the tone for the initial meeting and affect receptivity moving forward.

Other priorities can seem more pressing than choosing the right messenger. Meeting agendas, deadlines, or presentation content can overshadow dynamics related to messenger selection. Sometimes team leaders don't scrutinize decisions about who is speaking unless there is an issue on the line.

"It saves time and gives your ideas more consideration if you network to the person of authority for whom your idea has relevance and weight."

Rachel Hutchinson former VP Global Social Impact for Blackbaud

---

Deciding who attends meetings, who talks, and what they say depends on the stage of the relationship, who else is in the room, and how the relationship is going. Everyone wants to be the messenger who delivers good news. When the situation is unfavorable, few volunteers step forward. Either way, who speaks can be the difference between a catastrophe or a deft pivot. A strategically-selected messenger ensures that communication is heard and received as well as possible. Ultimately, the right messenger paired with a strategic message increases your chances of improving the growth of the relationship.

Beyond matching power to power in messenger selection, wise partnership builders also match expertise to expertise both in type of expertise and level of expertise. They don't send representatives to address specialized knowledge that isn't in their wheelhouse. One of my most successful team members at

World Vision never participated on an introductory call without a subject matter expert. This enabled him to match a partner's expertise while allowing him to do his job well, read the room and move the conversation along. He empowered his subject matter experts to discuss information with their respective counterparts rather than try to be the authority or act as the mouthpiece for every communication. Bringing other team members into the relationship in this way requires careful orchestration to ensure everyone can articulate the partnership's big picture goals, but it pays off.

"Make relationships with stickiness. Have a lot of touch points and people involved to make multi-faceted, rich, and long-term partnerships."

Raymond King President and CEO, Zoo Atlanta and former SVP Community Affairs, SunTrust Banks, Inc.

Here is more guidance on choosing the right messengers:

Experts. Don't try to be the expert when you aren't the expert. Doing so risks you coming off as a knowledgeable lightweight, not a well-yoked partner. Let legal staff address legal questions, program people answer program questions, and communications staff brief on their areas of expertise. You may occasionally be able to cover high level conversations, but you'll look silly if someone asks a deeper question that you can't answer. Encouraging subject matter experts to talk to each other has the added benefit of adding additional points of affinity with the partner.

Power to Power. Make sure CEOs talk to partner CEOs at key junctures. This matches political weight when it counts. At the beginning, this demonstrates commitment from the top and respect for the partner's senior leadership. After a deal is struck or at milestones, this contact shows continued support and appreciation. Finally, whenever a big problem arises, involve senior leadership in conversation about remedies. Again, this shows respect and underscores that the relationship is highly valued. At the same time, beware of overuse of your CEO. You may create a long list of new best friends for your CEO that he or she may have little time to maintain.

Leverage Trust. Connect respected and influential friends and acquaintances when appropriate. You need to be a good relationship mapper to do this well. Find out who in your organization or on your board knows someone of influence in partner organizations. A note or a call from a respected friend about an opportunity can generate momentum as relationships launch, evolve, and hit rough patches.

Gatekeeper Care. Take good care of the administrative staff. They exert influence with their bosses. If you make them feel inferior or take them for granted, you'll likely pay a price.

Training. Don't put people in an uncomfortable position. Some CEOs are great at operations, but sales conversations aren't their thing. Or programming specialists could be great at talking about their particular program area but not comfortable speaking with funders. I was once asked to serve on a board largely composed of IT experts because they needed someone who could help them communicate to non-IT types.

This next thought might come across like I'm talking out of both sides of my mouth. Yes, you need to pick the right messenger for specific communications, but you also need a united messaging front. Everyone who represents your organization must speak with one voice about the goals of the relationship. One team member can inadvertently derail progress by raising an unrelated concern. I've traveled to showcase projects for prospective funders just to have the plan fall apart when one person didn't stay on message. The prospective partner asked a local staff person what they most needed, and they replied that they specifically needed printers and another computer. That need was real, but we had bigger ideas at play. We ended up receiving technical hardware instead of a sought after building. We all learned from that. The next go around with a different funder, we ended up with a building.

To prevent poor outcomes, an account manager must oversee messaging closely. They need to keep up with all conversations in play. Staff tasked with any kind of partner communication need to know the bigger picture and how they fit into it. This allows them to answer questions appropriately and in sync with the overall plan and team. I'm not saying that people shouldn't speak their minds. Diversity of thought can bring the best to partnerships, but choosing the right time and place matters. To use an orchestra metaphor, selections often include solos, but they are rehearsed ahead of time, each musician knows when the solos are coming, and the conductor leads the performance.

Reflections

When have you seen an important message delivered by the wrong person? What happened, and how could the outcome have been different if a different person had been involved?

When have you seen someone experiencing a "fish out of water" moment in a meeting? Maybe they were asked something they didn't know or could not answer clearly. How could you have prevented that situation?

SPEAK YOUR PARTNER'S LANGUAGE

—

Consider carefully the language you use. I'm not talking about French or English, nor am I talking about avoiding salty sailor language. I have participated in meetings where English speakers spoke too fast and with unclear jargon for those whose native language wasn't English. This complicates any language barrier and can lead partners to miss important points. They might smile uncomfortably while struggling to understand, and you can come off as rude when you miss those nonverbal cues. This does not promote trust and respect. So, yes, I'm talking about that kind of language, too.

Let's consider jargon, which can feel like a language all its own and exclude people in conversations. No one wants to feel left behind. Children International used so many acronyms and code words that we literally created our own glossary. I took six months to learn the language with the glossary firmly in hand. The jargon was so second nature to long-time staff that they had difficulty keeping it out of conversations. You can't expect people from outside the organization to keep up when we use such internal speak. This isn't just a nonprofit issue. Companies rely on their own internal language, too. Using such language makes people feel like outsiders. Unable to follow the conversation, they feel alienated when you actually need them to feel comfortable and open to opportunities.

To some degree, using your own special language has benefits. Bankers are going to talk like bankers. People of faith often reference scripture and spiritual practice. People with a passion for a cause will embed their conversation with terms relevant to their work. Remember the story about my staff person who was "all Wall Street-y" in word, tone, and dress? He just couldn't talk to the hippy. One time, my own kids told me to stop talking like an executive. I didn't even know I was speaking weirdly in their eyes (and worse: in front of their friends). I was ordering at a fast food window, but apparently I did it oddly in their eyes. Trust doesn't bloom well when language feels odd and unfamiliar.

Learning another language is difficult, but making use of choice words common to your partner's world will build bridges and help with understanding. This doesn't alter what you have to say or offer. It is serving your content up on familiar plates. Be easy to understand, and you will develop relationships more easily.

Reflections ─────────────────────────────

Have you ever felt lost in a conversation because someone used terms you didn't know?

Have you taken the time to learn new jargon before meetings? How did that impact the conversation and the relationship?

─────────────────────────────

ANTICIPATE DISRUPTIONS AND PIVOT TOGETHER

—

No matter how hard you try, you can't avoid disruptions that challenge partnerships. Such headwinds can involve stock market disruptions as well as shifts in competitive environments (e.g., Amazon offering health services or their rapidly increasing share of the package delivery business, currently a quarter of all deliveries). Disruptions also arise from internal shifts in business strategies, departmental reorganization, and staff turnover. If you are tied to a company whose business model is becoming obsolete (think video rentals or brick-and-mortar banking), you'll probably feel the pain of a lost partnership unless you pivot as the company maneuvers to regain its marketplace footing. Nonprofits that can demonstrate alignment with the company's new strategy not only have a good chance of saving their relationship, but they will have also earned more respect from the company.

Disruptions can also strike nonprofits in ways that require corporate partners to pivot. One of the biggest disruptions in recent times was the pandemic. Children International had to change direction quickly when COVID necessitated the shuttering of all their facilities. They masterfully shifted to telehealth and food provision to serve the most urgent needs where they had a presence. They also strategically communicated with individual, foundation, and corporate partners to enroll their support in new ways. CI actually secured funding increases for special needs like technology. Companies and major individual donors valued the transparent communication and the nonprofit's quick workarounds. This built even more trust and led to greater investment in innovation to meet the demands of that time.

Yes, profits and nonprofits face disruptions all the time. How you deal with them can build or erode your relationships. One sector that was hit especially hard during the pandemic was the airline industry. Delta Air Lines was at their peak right before the pandemic, positioned as the top revenue-generating airline in the world. They had just made the biggest employee profit-sharing payout in airline history of $1.6 billion. According to the documentary *The Steepest Climb*, Delta CEO Ed Bastian was called by the President of the United States on March 11, 2020, and told that all European travel must be suspended due to the pandemic. In a normal spring, Delta would book $150 million in a day, but in less than a week, its bookings fell to under $9 million a day. Life could not have changed more for the airline. That documentary tells the inspiring story of Delta's leadership and the faith the company's employees demonstrated.

I want to examine a part of the Delta story that didn't make it into that documentary because it offers a valuable lesson regarding partner reaction when disruption arises. Delta has an admirable reputation for supporting causes; however, when revenues took that pandemic hit, the company had to scrutinize all costs not directly associated with staying afloat. Of course, this included a pause on philanthropy, which was hard for partner nonprofits that were also in crisis mode. Some of those nonprofits responded with empathy for Delta amidst their own fears. Some nonprofits, however, responded negatively—even angrily. We are all human and respond to crises in different ways. How you respond to another's pain, especially in the midst of your own pain, reveals a lot about character. Character influences a relationship.

As with Delta and many others, you often can't fix your partners' problems when they experience disruptions. You should show empathy and look at pausing or even sunsetting the relationship if such a move would be helpful. Such selflessness is remembered and further deepens trust, lasting well after the partnership ends.

That was a rather extreme example. Most disruptions aren't nearly that dramatic. You can anticipate some disruptions if you pay attention and communicate often. Anticipating a challenge provides opportunities to modify agreements so you stay synced to your partner's reality. Make the effort to stay abreast of trends that might negatively affect your partners. Set up Google alerts with keywords and partner names so you'll know when they appear in the news. Ask your research teams to track data related to your partner's business. Read up on topics that might not be central to your world but might help you see a future opportunity or concern for your partners. I like to read futurists' writings about trends. I'm sometimes surprised at their predictions, but making the effort to stay current has allowed me to initiate useful conversations with partners. The display of genuine concern and interest helps build affinity.

Aside from all that, your best strategy for anticipating surprises and giving your organization time to adjust to disruptions is regular communication with your partners. Every time you meet for updates, ask them about their world. Bring up data or news you've read that might impact them. This conversation may generate more useful information, and it helps them see you as a genuinely concerned partner. You want them to know that you are continually looking for ways to enhance the partnership and for win/win scenarios.

Best efforts to anticipate and proactively respond to change don't always work out. Remember the TOMS story? Their business model was disrupted when other retailers copied their "buy one, give one" shoe promotion. The novel approach lost its novelty and failed to drive sales. They were struggling, and their nonprofit partners couldn't do much to help. TOMS had to adjust their strategy to meet the changing market dynamics, and Children International's partnership no longer fit. Try as we did, we just couldn't find a way to align with their new strategy. We parted ways but with great appreciation for what we had accomplished together. I am certain that if CI proposed an idea that did fit TOMS' goals, they would have embraced CI again as a partner.

Make it easier to navigate unavoidable disruptions by giving preference to partners who welcome growing pains and create pivots that offer mutual benefit. This brings to mind the AVIV Foundation, likely the best partner I ever worked with from this perspective. They not only monitored the market conditions that were creating waves for their grantees, but they also approached everyone with grace and empathy. They encouraged creativity and strategic shifts when scenarios merited them. The foundation valued being kept in the loop as Children International discerned the best ways to navigate COVID challenges. They were excited to hear about pivots like turning to telemedicine and food deliveries to serve the most vulnerable children and families. The foundation's leaders treated their partners with the utmost respect and honored their expertise and commitment to creating good. They especially respected the transparent communication and reasoned approach CI took to solving problems.

Reflections

When has a partnership you've been a part of experienced disruption? How did the partners' leaders adjust to the changes?

Think of a partnership that successfully pivoted with changing times. What was behind the success?

Chapter 6

———

EMBRACE
THE MAGIC OF
SOFT STUFF

I n this book and others about partnerships, you'll find tips galore and checklists to help you build successful partnerships. Experts can help you learn everything from negotiation skills and fair value exchange to reporting and stewardship. All of this is vital to becoming an effective leader in the partnership arena, but there is more to it. The most successful partnership builders rely on more than skilled staff, effective processes, and strategies. They rely on the "soft stuff."

This involves more than just people skills, which are certainly essential. Partnership leaders must be adept at people skills like shaking hands properly, looking people in the eye, and exercising sensitivity to body language. The soft stuff I'm focusing on goes beyond that and addresses a host of others: serendipity, courage, faith, and something I call "being versus doing." Teams with these less traditional characteristics outperform those that lack them. Soft stuff may be hard to measure, but you recognize it when you see it, especially in the ROI of teams that embody it.

"75 percent of long-term job success depends on people skills, while only 25 percent relies on technical knowledge."

Peggy Klaus executive coach and author of *The Hard Truth about Soft Skills*

COURAGE FUELED BY PURPOSE

Courage is not only soft stuff, it is a shapeshifter. It looks different in different situations and can be big or small. Regardless of the size of the act of courage, it can create ripples beyond what anyone can anticipate. A great partnership builder exercises the courage to take calculated risks. These can include political, economic, or even physical risks. People who act courageously and succeed are applauded. They can also bear withering criticism when confronted by disappointing results. In my experience, calculated courage is a prized attribute to be celebrated.

Here is a small act of courage that had a big ripple. I was trying to meet with the CEO of Interbrand. His company had worked up brand valuations for the likes of Coca-Cola. I was with the American Cancer Society, and we needed to know our brand's worth to support more robust partner conversations.

He seemed interested in helping us, an interest partly grounded in business and partly grounded in a personal rationale. From a business perspective, such valuations had never been calculated for nonprofits. Conducting one for ACS could potentially generate business from other large nonprofits. The personal appeal came from a story shared by so many of us: his family was touched by cancer. He drew a straight line between helping the organization attract more support and helping to find a cure.

Unfortunately, that CEO went quiet on me. He didn't return my calls or emails. I hate when people ghost me. I began to fear that perhaps his interest had waned or the original indications weren't as strong as I had thought.

After a few weeks, I found myself shopping in a stationery store and saw a blank card with the picture on the front of a grown lion being bitten in the butt by a baby lion. I bought the card and penned a witty apology for "being a pain in the rear" for calling so much. I also shared my conviction that we could help more people battle cancer if we could continue our conversation. I received a quick call back with a roar of laughter. . . and a meeting on the books.

Some people raised their eyebrows when I shared what I had done. They thought it was risky, even borderline unprofessional. Perhaps it was, but the brand valuation we received helped ACS build a number of relationships with large companies. My small act of courage generated a helpful ripple.

A much bigger act of courage involved a friend of mine, Farhan Irshad, and his discussions with the Taliban. When he worked for Save the Children in Afghanistan, the Taliban shut down their microloan program, designed to assist women in economically depressed areas start businesses. The program helped families emerge from poverty. Unfortunately, continuing the program in light of a Taliban prohibition endangered many people. Most organizations would have shuttered the program under these circumstances. Instead, my friend took the gutsy step to request a meeting with the local Taliban leader. When they met, he assured the leader that the program was properly aligned with local customs. Essentially, women applied for loans in the company of male family members and for business opportunities that were consistent with culturally accepted roles for women. My friend exhibited fortitude, optimism, and conviction to initiate that conversation. His initiative could have been interpreted as a challenge. Instead, the result was amazing. The mutual respect that came from that meeting allowed Save the Children to continue providing microloans.

Another example of courageous action is found in the story previously shared about Citibank offering $150,000 to the American Cancer Society for use of their marks on credit cards. It was tempting to take the money and move on. Asking for a delay to determine the appropriate cost could have prompted the company to turn to another nonprofit. Fortunately, both ACS and Citibank were curious, courageous, and motivated by fairness. These soft attributes led to negotiating a proportionate value for tapping ACS assets.

A different kind of courage was described earlier in the book about the staff and volunteers of Children International in Honduras. In the face of closing physical centers during COVID, the team was determined to continue serving children and their families with what they needed most: hope, medical advice, and food. To buy food, they reallocated money that had been used to operate the center, but they faced two other obstacles. CI didn't have trucks, and safety was a concern in heavily gang-controlled areas. They needed partners. The local government had trucks, and the Catholic church was respected by the gangs—voila! Everyone united to make this three-way partnership work. Their courage to think differently, to reach out to others, and to try a novel approach enabled them to provide food where it was desperately needed.

"Courage is the most important of all virtues because without courage, you can't practice any other virtue consistently"

Maya Angelou author, poet, and civil rights activist

Sometimes, courage comes in the form of bucking mainstream thought leaders. I ran into this when we built the first incentive plan for individual and team rewards related to corporate partnerships at the American Cancer Society. The idea was roundly criticized as inappropriate for nonprofits. The Association for Fundraising Professionals stood against incentives, a position I thought was wrong. Incentives work in the corporate sector. Surely we could devise an appropriate way to try it in the nonprofit sector. Thanks to our external experts at Ernst & Young, we created a plan that navigated internal and external concerns and pressed forward. Using the word "bonus" instead of "incentive" and basing it on team effort in addition to individual effort were the keys. Our idea worked well and inspired staff to ramp up their performance. Incentive plans are now commonplace in the nonprofit sector.

Can you handle one more story of courage? The courage here was in a nonprofit's conviction and persistence to stand with an idea they knew to be bold. Corporate resistance softened with time, but at the start of the story, the nonprofit's proposal was not well received. The company made bras and other undergarments for women. Komen's leadership felt confident that a pink ribbon on a popular bra would be the perfect place for messaging to women about the advantages of early breast cancer detection. Almost all women wear bras, and, increasingly, they talked about cancer, so it made sense to Komen. Hang tags on bras would be a great place to present information to women about self-exams, mammograms, and sources for cancer information. The idea wasn't one-sided. Komen had initiated similar promotions with other companies and had seen increased sales. The evidence strongly suggested that this idea was transferable to the bra business, too.

Unfortunately, the idea of associating bras with breast cancer didn't sound smart to the company. They were supportive of the cause but felt that the specter of breast cancer might dampen consumer interest at the point of purchase. They did not want to risk suppressing sales. As time moved on and public discourse about breast cancer evolved, the growing passion for finding a cure became hard to ignore. Eventually, the company's position shifted, and they found the courage to add a pink ribbon to the bra along with early detection information. As Komen had predicted, the move boosted business. Patience, conviction, and courage generated benefits for the company, the nonprofit, and women!

Reflections

When have you shown courage in a partner situation? How did it alter the trajectory?

When have you seen the need for greater courage in a situation? How might you help people develop much-needed courage?

SERENDIPITY

Everyone has experienced coincidences that seem too strange to be accidental. We often chalk them up to chance or serendipity. I talked about some of that while describing how my career seemed to have an uncanny evolution not of my making. I love serendipitous happenings. I believe they are gifts, part of the magic of the universe. Serendipity can play a beautiful part in any relationship, including partnerships.

Here is a simple example of the blessing behind a serendipitous moment. I ran into a friend at a hardware store. We had not talked in years. She lived in a different city five hours away. I was in that store on a whim, just searching for a picture hanger for my new office. When we saw each other, our mouths gaped open in surprise, and we embraced. We paused our busy lives and learned that we were both in states of good transition. Then, we had what my daughters call a "jinx" moment. We said the same words at the same time, "even a good transition creates stress." Our reconnection and hugs offered an emotional boost that each of us needed right then.

So what does that have to do with partnerships? I've seen it play out in that arena, too. I remember trying hard to arrange a meeting with someone just to find that I was seated near her at an event, a dinner I hadn't originally planned to attend. Another time, one of my friends landed a new job in a company I wanted to partner with. Another friend shared a story about her child ending up on the same sports team as the child of a person heading up one of her key accounts. And what about airports: such great places for serendipity! I have run into many people at airports at the most opportune times. The key is to not just be open to serendipity, but to anticipate it. Enjoy the moments when they happen and create magic from them.

These kinds of stories do make for good cocktail party conversation, but I invite you to think about them more deeply. What might you create from an unexpected encounter? Maybe you will have the chance to buoy another person's life for a moment, be it in a business or personal way. But really, aren't relationships just one big bucket of love and humanity? As Steven Covey said, "We don't have a business life and a personal one." We have one life, and we have the chance to sow magic wherever we focus.

Shifting back to partnership examples: Remember the story about Vaseline and Direct Relief? Unilever didn't conduct exhaustive research to find Direct Relief. One of their team members heard a news interview with frontline medical volunteers who happened to be touting the value of Vaseline for wound treatment. They were Direct Relief volunteers. Instead of simply enjoying the unexpected story about a product she worked on and letting it pass, she shared the story with her colleagues. This prompted an internal conversation and led them to Direct Relief. Serendipity was the start of this great partnership.

"Sometimes life drops blessings in your lap without you lifting a finger."

Charlton Heston actor

A serendipitous encounter during my Honduras mission trip led to unexpected partnership conversations. The leader of our group has been hosting these trips for decades as part of his faith journey. The trips enable his friends and associates to directly witness the impressive work that lifts kids out of poverty. Shortly before our trip, something uncanny happened. He was reluctantly taking an online exercise class recommended by his doctor. None of the half-a-dozen people in the class knew each other, and they lived in different cities across the world. He casually mentioned in a class that he would miss their next session because he was traveling to Honduras. One of the other exercisers shared that she would be in the country, too. How unlikely! Ever ready to share his passion for the work there, he invited her to our group's closing dinner. Here's the kicker: she was the U.S. ambassador to Honduras! Because she joined us, representatives from USAID took an interest in the program, too. I don't know if it has led to funding yet, but I bet it will.

Another story of chance is from my time with Women for Women International (WfWI). They work with women who have been victims of war, some of the most courageous women I have ever met. WfWI offers these seemingly broken women a year-long program to heal emotionally and economically. It helps them regain respect, dignity, and a sense of value. Part of the reality of this program is that the countries they work in are fragile. Sometimes, bringing partners to see the program in person and witness the remarkable resilience of these determined women is simply not safe.

One such country is the Democratic Republic of Congo. Since I was finishing up a trip in neighboring Rwanda, my boss asked me to make a site visit and assess whether our locations in the DRC were safe enough for partners and donors. The visit went well, safety protocols were strong, and I met several inspiring women. All went well until I was ready to leave. I made a mistake, likely rooted in the language barrier. My driver and I had developed a combination of gestures and broken English to communicate during my visit. On our last trip together, we neared the one-lane wooden bridge that crosses a river at the DRC border with Rwanda. I used gestures to ask if I could take a picture of the interesting bridge. He nodded and smiled.

As I lifted my phone and took a picture, the border control officers stepped in front of our vehicle and surrounded the car. They pulled me from the car and confiscated my phone. Suddenly, everyone was talking loudly and pointing for us to turn around and go back. I was allowed back in the car, and several officers walked alongside the car as we slowly made our way to the border control office. My nervous driver gestured for me to stay put while he went inside. I assumed he was trying to explain the situation. I focused on my hands to avoid the hard stares outside the window. That was likely the longest ten minutes of my life.

When my driver returned, he wasn't smiling and said, "You go. You sorry, my friend." I wasn't sure what he meant. I walked across the street by myself through a parting sea of people. The person in charge was visibly unhappy. He shook my phone at me and shouted, "No pictures!" several times. For some reason, I bowed like I was back in Japan and repeated "very sorry" what seemed like a hundred times. I then said, "Please delete" several times as I pointed to the phone. He calmed down and let me delete the picture. After an awkward pause, I gave him almost all the money I had. He returned my phone and permitted me to leave. With wobbly legs, I made my way back to the car, and we drove over the bridge. I later found out that the border crossing supervisor that day had been a schoolmate of my driver. I'm not sure this story would have ended the same way had they not known each other.

Serendipity didn't end there. My seatmate on the plane out of Rwanda asked me if I was OK. I guess I looked a little rattled. Come to find out, they worked for the Mennonite Foundation and had also just returned from the DRC. They were exploring funding opportunities there—for programs just like ours. What are the odds?

Reflections ——————————————————————————

When have you experienced chance moments that have led to
something wonderful for you or someone else?

Have you ever let a serendipitous moment pass and wondered
what might have come of it had you leaned into that moment?

——————————————————————————————————

SILVER LININGS

—

Good can often come from bad. Given the complexity of
partnership-building, constant change, and all the internal and
external stakeholders involved, you can usually count on something not going as planned. Even so, I have always found posi-
tives associated with both minor and major bumps in the road.

People who can spot silver linings have a better chance of
maintaining equanimity in a relationship and creating posi-
tives out of less-than-ideal circumstances. In a physical disaster, wise people implore us to look for the helpers, to draw inspiration from them, and to join them however we can. This is
true across all difficulties. Shine a light on what is good to help
build from there.

When you work in partnership-building, this ability to discern good and to inspire creative pivots can be a powerful attribute. This perspective is more than just assuming the best
in people as opposed to finding fault. I believe we can create
good from whatever challenging hand we are dealt. We start by
assessing our situation and looking for the upsides amidst the
failure and weakness.

When COVID hit, the world turned upside down for most companies and nonprofits. Children International's model of lifting kids out of poverty was based on offering services to them from the safety of centers built in densely populated, urban slums. As I mentioned before, the pandemic shuttered the centers. Instead of halting all operations, CI evaluated their capabilities and devised a pivot. They found silver linings in their technology and excellent IT support. Thanks to this, CI employees—even the huge call center in the U.S.—began working from home within weeks of the shutdown. Globally, they shifted to strategies like telehealth and remote education for children living in poverty. Their tenacity and boldness won them new partnerships with technology companies and generous donors to expand the availability of computer tablets for children. Many of the children had been trying to keep up in class using the family phone or one borrowed from neighbors. Studying by phone was problematic on many levels. The tablets were a huge blessing.

Another silver lining was that this disruption spurred CI to rethink everything, including paper-based systems that had been in place for decades. Their main revenue model was child sponsorship. Physical letters exchanged between children and sponsors were key to their emotional bond, the foundation of their sponsorship giving. The new difficulty in collecting, vetting, and delivering letters spurred CI to test electronic messaging. This turned out to be faster, easier, and less expensive. They found solutions to address privacy concerns. Electronic communication between children and sponsors has continued to evolve, one of many silver linings that arose from the pandemic and continues to deliver positive outcomes.

Another example of silver linings involves a friend of mine who worked for Save the Children. He is naturally wired to find the good in challenging situations, which served him especially well when he was stationed in Afghanistan. As a member of an international group there, he had to lodge in local rather than international housing because he is of Pakistani heritage. Of course, it seemed unfair. Local housing didn't have the "comforts" of international housing, a rather generous way to describe the contrast. Rather than harbor resentment, he embraced the housing situation and discovered advantages that positively impacted his mission there.

In the local housing, he became privy to information that was unavailable to those in the international house, where details were so sanitized that certain problems were almost invisible to them. Staying among the local staff, my friend lived closer to truths that sparked creative discussions. These conversations, combined with his commitment to collaborative solutions, helped him build relationships that other international staff could not. He was able to paint a more complete picture for his international colleagues, allowing everyone to contribute their strengths to planning in relevant ways. The less comfortable lodging was well worth the sacrifice to him. In fact, he feels that all the challenges he has encountered throughout his career have contributed to shaping him as a leader who is particularly suited to co-create benefits from difficulties.

I share his belief that all our experiences can be used to prepare us to uniquely engage our present and future situations. I mentioned that I grew up in a military family, which required us to uproot and move every three years. Elements of that life were hard. I'm sure it wasn't easy for my parents, either. Each time we relocated, I grew stronger at making new friends and more comfortable figuring out the ropes of new places. I cultivated more confidence than I even realized. Moving around the world as a young person shaped me in beautiful ways. For example, I don't buy into stereotypes of other cultures, which allows me to see people for who they are as individuals. I also observe behavior and read people beyond what their words say. I think this helps me get to know people. If I see them in this way, I can hear them. If I hear them, we can learn from each other and work together to create a better impact. Looking back, I believe this nomadic lifestyle was the best "worst" thing that ever happened to me.

Reflections

What have been your brightest silver linings found in difficult situations?

How has finding and focusing on the silver linings benefited you and others?

VALUE OF A CONNECTOR

—

I wish I had done a better job throughout my career of keeping up with friends and associates. I was privileged to meet wonderful people over the years, but when I moved or changed jobs, I didn't always maintain connections. My attention focused on my transition. If they weren't part of the new adventure, they weren't top of mind, and I often didn't reach out to them enough to keep the relationship alive. In my defense, maintaining close contact wasn't as easy before cell phones and social media.

This is really important when you recognize that partnerships don't exist without relationships between people, and relationships atrophy when neglected. If you struggle to maintain relationships, perhaps you share my excuses. My biggest one is singular focus. I am good at focusing intently on whatever captures my passion at any one time. Unfortunately, this exclusive focus can block out anything unrelated to my current goal. I see this as the opposite of silver linings. It is the fly in the ointment, some yuck with the good stuff. This particular weakness has caused me to miss out on valuable opportunities. I deal with this kind of yuck similarly to how I deal with the good stuff: see the lesson in it and move forward.

Realistically, we can't stay in touch with everyone. No one has that kind of time. We can, however, take time to write notes or make calls to those with whom we feel a genuine connection. Do this with no particular agenda in mind. Definitely call when you have a lead or a brilliant idea for them, but let check-ins focus generally on how they're doing. Your call might uncover ways you could help or perhaps how someone you know could be a godsend for them. This purposeful conversation is that of a caring connector.

The fun of staying in touch and rejuvenating relationships is a wonderful byproduct of being a great connector. Staying relevant in people's lives, especially if you can help from time to time, feels great, too. If you are top of mind, people will also contact you to share with you. This reciprocity just feels good.

Over time, people who reach out to friends regularly and connect with others expand their circles. More than casual friends, these are people who care about each other. In my opinion, these circles equate to much more than "networks." They are very different from our LinkedIn networks. Although I have a ton of those connections—technically my network—I couldn't pick most of them out of a crowd.

"The best relationship builders connect with, invest in, observe well, and personalize their relationships. This approach leads to being relationally rich."

Glen Jackson Co-founder of Jackson Spalding Public Relations

The world is a small place. Connectors help make it even smaller. Their efforts to stay in touch and to express genuine interest in others often lead to meaningful opportunities. You can easily do this. Just a few phone calls each week can be an investment in unexpected surprises. When you think of someone because they might prove helpful to another person, take that moment to connect them. Anything can happen as a result. Perhaps you reach out and find that someone has moved and is trying to find a new job, dentist, daycare, or hairdresser. When you help them, they remember you for it.

I knew a senior United Way leader who made a point of contacting all the new corporate CEOs in his area with the simple agenda of welcoming them and offering to introduce them to other local CEOs and influencers. They remembered him for this helpful offer. When he needed them later on, they were eager to assist. Helping people is the right thing to do—and smart. Some-day, when you have a need, you can feel confident about lifting the phone to talk about it. You won't have to say, "Remember me? We haven't talked in five years, but I have this problem . . ."

One of the best people I know at nurturing relationships and connecting people is my long-time friend, Ken Bernhardt. He is Regents Professor of Marketing Emeritus at Georgia State Univer-sity and seems to remember every student he ever taught. They remember him, too! He has served on numerous boards and has been a valued advisor to large and small companies and numer-ous nonprofits. He doesn't talk to all his connections all the time, but when he does reach out, he offers something meaningful to them. When Ken calls, people want to know what he has to say, and they appreciate hearing from him.

Reflections

What benefit do you see from connecting people with each other, whether or not you derive a benefit?

When has being a connector brought you an unanticipated benefit?

USE ALL YOUR STRENGTH

In the book *The Dance of Hope,* author Bill Frey tells a beau-tiful story of his growing up in Georgia. He had tried his best to dig out the roots of a dead tree from the stubborn red clay

Georgians both love and hate. (I know because I am an often frustrated gardener in Georgia, too.) After Frey exhausts himself trying everything to remove the stump, his father tells him he isn't using all his strength. This comment made him angry. After cooling down, Frey asks his dad what he meant. His father simply replies that Frey hadn't asked him for help yet. When you ask for help, you begin to use all your strength.

That story connects perfectly to partnership-building. Here are a few takeaways about working with other people to use their strength along with your own:

- Complex partnerships never succeed with one person talking to just one other person. It takes a team effort, with each member doing their part well.

- Partnership building at its best is characterized by people strong enough to be vulnerable, and strong enough to open up about what they really need. When you open up, you allow people to offer talents or connections you didn't know about.

- Grace and accountability are important to empowering everyone to go the extra mile. Dealing with inevitable stumbles together results in faster recoveries. This compassionate accountability is an approach that taps extra strength.

- Big egos and partnership building don't jibe. Oversized egos, blinded by their own glow, don't see all that others bring to the table; therefore, they can't harness all their team's strengths. These egos can also be fragile, puffed up one minute and bruised the next. Be the person that draws people in and inspires them to join the team so that you can draw on everyone's skills. This requires humility.

• Never stop listening or applauding. Such actions encourage people and draw out more of their ideas and talents. Discover and use all the strengths available to your team.

• Use the term "team" loosely. Some of the people with keys to unlocking opportunities don't attend weekly meetings or participate in negotiations. The friend that helped me secure time with the brand manager at General Mills played the biggest individual role related to that success. All of your relationships comprise your strength. Nurture them and invite them to join your journey.

Reflections

When have you "gone it alone" and succeeded? Who could have helped you succeed even more?

When you have failed, who might have helped you win? Or, if triumph wasn't in the cards, who could help you process the failure in a way that creates good out of bad?

BEING-VERSUS-DOING

—

When all the "soft things" I've discussed are present in someone, you are likely looking at one of the most successful people in the business. These pros don't operate like this only during business hours. They strive to embody the soft stuff all the time because that is how they are wired. They couldn't disable their soft skills even if they wanted to. This is the essence of being- versus-doing.

Being-versus-doing is an aspiration to strive for all the time. When you come from this place, you believe that life offers you opportunities that surpass your current needs. This orientation calls you to lean into situations where positive outcomes are not automatic.

The people who are the best at partnerships are "always on," continually looking at the world through an optimistic lens and seeking greater good. They identify ripe opportunities in some of the most challenging situations—and with some of the most challenging people. They seek to understand their own motivation and to know what other people need. They really see people. From this comes bold energy, ideas, and creativity. When that is aimed at a plan for mutual success, magic does indeed happen. Whether it is family connections, friendships, or business relationships, the best partnership builders look at the world like this all the time. It is who they are, not just what they do.

Make no mistake, these people aren't "Pollyanna" push-overs. I think they are what the Bible calls "shrewd and innocent," masterful at understanding complicated situations, motivations, and needs. With this knowledge, they devise clever ways forward while remaining pure of heart and intent. Farhan Irshad gained a global reputation for his ability to address situations that seemed unfixable to most people at Save the Children. His approach for resolving such complexities involved this balance of wisdom, creative thinking, and pure intent—

sprinkled with a whole lot of courage and respect for others. I don't see myself as having mastered being-versus-doing on Farhan's level, but I am dedicated to continuing to grow for as long as I am here.

For me, the state of being-versus-doing involves beliefs and faith. I don't actively promote one religious structure over another, but I believe the commonality among religious beliefs invites us to be kind to one another and to help the least, last, and lost among us. This is how we can all contribute to a greater good. If we check in regularly with this universal aspiration, we can be powerful together. Tapping into a source that transcends our individual selves allows us to co-create more than we can possibly imagine on our own.

When I worked with my World Vision team to set revenue goals, after all the number crunching and account analysis was done, I'd ask them to pause for God space. With all you know and all you think you can do, where does your spirit tell you things can go? What is possible if you are being rather than doing this job. I asked them to be open to having their plans be influenced—if not driven—by a force bigger than themselves. You can ask yourself that, too, whatever your goals may be. After that reflection, step into your journey again and know you aren't alone.

Another way to think about being-versus-doing is to consider a role where being is paramount. Picture great moms and dads. They are never off duty, no matter how old their kids are. They are forever a parent, and a part of them is always tuned to the well-being of their children. This is an orientation you can bring to any role, be it personal or professional.

Reflections

What positive aspect of you is "always on?" How has that created good around you?

Given that what you focus on grows, what do you want to focus on as an element of your being-versus-doing?

How could being-versus-doing create beneficial changes in your life?

PASSION

—

Contagious passion is another key attribute of the best partnership builders. You don't go the extra mile for something you don't believe in. You do that for what speaks to your passion in life.

I joined Children International largely because of the passion I witnessed in John Clause. He had been my boss at World Vision, and I could feel his love for children in our very first conversation. He did not view his work helping impoverished children as merely a job. This was his calling, and he wanted people on his team to share this passion, not merely for the organization, but for the kids. When he moved on from World Vision to Children International, he continued living this passion, and he made it contagious. I happily joined him once again to do this vital work.

John started a fire in me, but my own passion for helping children and families lift themselves out of poverty grew brightest when I met the local Children International staff and volunteers.

In most cases, the volunteers were women who were the mothers and aunts of the children they were helping. CI wasn't just a job to them, it was personal. They believed CI programs provided a pathway because they saw kids emerge from poverty due directly to this assistance. Their work and volunteer efforts aimed to create a better life for their children. This collective selflessness focused not on their advancement but on the benefits for the next generation. Their passion was fueled more by every success. They saw kids growing healthy, building confidence, and realizing dreams of formal employment. If John's passion was contagious, their passion was unstoppable.

The only place I have felt similar passion was in the eyes of the beneficiaries of Women for Women International's programs. They are survivors of war, and their spirits are also unstoppable. My passion became so deep that I couldn't tell their courageous stories without shedding tears. Thinking of their commitment and spirit, I still cry when I consider their perilous journeys in contrast to the comfort of my own privilege. Their courage is unmatched, as is their commitment to creating better futures for their families. What is even more inspiring is that their passion creates a ripple effect generationally. May we all pursue such love and passion. It moves mountains.

Reflections

What are you passionate about? How does it show up in your life? How can you make it more prominent in your life?

How have other people you have known or read about harnessed their passion? What grew from their focus?

HUMOR

OK, that all got a bit heavy. Let's lighten up. People learn in different ways. Some are visual, some are kinesthetic, and some operate with a combination of modalities. Some of us learn better from mistakes than from successes, and some of us remember things better if we connect emotions to our learning, like pain or joy. All of that helps us learn, but let's also consider not taking ourselves too seriously. A sense of humor is healthy in this line of business. Even the most amazing among us make mistakes. Being able to laugh at yourself while you learn from your stubbed toes is a blessing. Seriously, I believe it is essential to learn from our mistakes, and I also believe that we shouldn't beat ourselves up too badly for them. This is why I choose to close the book with bloopers.

Below are some highlights of embarrassing moments. Some are mine, and others were shared by friends who I interviewed for this book. They are all real life stories—and most weren't funny when they happened! A bit of distance from some experiences helps, right? The people who offered these flubs did so with the understanding that they were learning opportunities, mixed in with giggles. Names have been withheld to prevent the snickers from reverberating back to the perpetrators of the goofs.

• Sitting in The Coca-Cola headquarters executive dining room with Bea Perez, guests are asked what they want to drink. One person quickly and automatically responds with their favorite beverage: tea. This person promptly flushed bright red and tried to rescind the order. Bea graciously waved away the faux pas

209

and insisted she have tea. She squirmed and drank tea while others enjoyed a refreshing Coca-Cola. I hated tea after that. Yes, that was me.

• Staff pore over a proposal for UPS for months. It is perfect! You want to ensure the materials arrive, so you ask your assistant to have the delivery tracked. The mailroom sends it via FedEx.

• You land a fantastic televised interview for your lead sponsor at a huge event. You are so proud of making that happen for them and just know they are going to love you for it. As you watch the broadcast, you see their main competitor's logo displayed prominently in the background. Ugh!

• How many potential partners have misspelled "Chick-fil-A"? Proofreading is an invaluable asset.

• Delta Air Lines is the main sponsor at an event, but you unwittingly raffle off Southwest Airlines tickets.

• You are talking candidly in an elevator about what didn't go swimmingly in a session with a big prospective partner. You aren't alone. A lady introduces herself as the admin for your key contact as she exits the elevator.

• Similar to the last one: you are on an airplane, discussing your strategy. You go to visit the bathroom and see people from a competing organization sitting within earshot.

• Your boss accompanies you to a meeting and asks you to drive. He is walking a bit ahead of you as you enter the building. You notice a Cheerio from your kid's in-car breakfast stuck to his butt. Do you try to brush it away? Always keep your car clean.

• You open your slide presentation, ready to wow the group, only to find a cute animated cat meowing on the cover slide. Never let your children near your laptop. OK, that was me, too.

• When AirTran was in business, the head of marketing and community engagement would receive out-of-town representatives from nonprofits seeking funding or flights. At the end of meetings, he would ask them what flight they were on so he could upgrade them to first class as a show of respect. More than a few visitors had flown in on a competitor airline.

• Zoom meetings are their own category of fun. Someone thought it would be a good idea to take the call (muted but unfortunately with video on) into the bathroom. You can't un-see that!

Reflections —————————

When have you seen humor dissolve tension in a meeting?
When has shifting your own perspective with levity
   changed your view and helped you take a more positive
   course of action?
What are the lessons from your bloopers?

AFTERWORD

Writing this book has been on my mind and heart for many years. It is my hope that the stories and insights shared here inspire today's partnership-builders to delve into conversations that allow them to explore relationship opportunities well beyond simple and obvious exchanges of value. May they find and harness the phenomenal power that is available through aligning assets and pain points for significant mutual gain, and may these efforts create great good in the world.

ACKNOWLEDGEMENTS

I am so very grateful to the many people who have helped me bring this book to life. Ken Bernhardt has been a constant source of encouragement and a great connector to many people who have kindly shared their experiences and expert knowledge with me. I am thankful for Ken's support and love. I am also deeply grateful to the Ripples Media publishing team, especially Jon Reese. Jon is an extraordinary editor, sounding board, and writing coach. I could not have produced this work without him.

The stories and insights shared in this book are derived from my own professional experience as well as from accounts shared by friends and acquaintances. My heartfelt gratitude goes out to the following circle of experts I had the pleasure of interviewing. Their wisdom is sprinkled throughout this book.

Ed Baker Professor, Georgia State University and former Publisher, *The Atlanta Business Chronicle*

Ken Bernhardt Consultant and Regents Professor of Marketing Emeritus, Georgia State University

Carol Cone CEO Carol Cone ON PURPOSE, former Chairman and Founder Cone LLC, and author of *Breakthrough Nonprofit Branding*

Ann Cramer Civic Leader, Community Volunteer, and Retired IBM Director Americas, Corporate Citizenship

Kathleen Dunlop CMO North American, Unilever Beauty and Wellness brands

Vicki Escarra Senior Advisor, Boston Consulting Group, former CMO, Delta Air Lines, and former CEO for Feeding America

Daryl Evans former VP Consumer Advertising and Marketing Communications, AT&T and former VP Strategic Sports Alliances, American Cancer Society

Karen Flanders Senior Consultant, Brand Culture Company, former Director of Sustainability, The Coca-Cola Company, and former Campaign Director, World Wildlife Fund.

Dick Greenly Board Chair, Water4 and Owner, Pumps of Oklahoma

John Hancock CEO, Junior Achievement of Georgia

Steve Hellen Head of Information Management of Geneva Center, Humanitarian Demining

Jo Ann Herold CEO, Herold Growth Consulting, former CMO Honeybaked Ham, former VP Brand Strategy Arby's, and Vice Chairman, Arby's Foundation

David Hessekiel former President, Engage for Good

ACKNOWLEDGEMENTS

Bob Hope Chairman, Hope Beckham Espinosa Public Relations

Rachel Hutchinson former VP Global Social Impact, Blackbaud

Tad Hutcheson Managing Director, Community Engagement, Delta Air Lines

Farhan Irshad Chairman of the Board, NetHope, former SVP and COO, HIAS and former Finance Director International Programs, Save the Children

Glen Jackson Co-founder, Jackson Spalding Public Relations

Raymond King President and CEO Zoo Atlanta and former SVP Community Affairs, SunTrust Banks, Inc.

Bryan Klopack Chief Growth Officer, Autism Speaks, former SVP, Reading is Fundamental, and former VP Corporate Alliances, Special Olympics International

Allison Kostiuk VP Client Engagement, Turnkey

Karl Lowe CIO, Catholic Relief Services

Scott McCune Founder, McCune Sports & Entertainment Ventures and former VP Global Partnerships and Experiential Marketing, The Coca-Cola Company

Katrina McGee EVP and CMO, American Heart Association

Hala Moddelmog CEO, Woodruff Arts Center, former President, Arby's Restaurant Group, and former President and CEO, Susan G. Komen for the Cure

William Pate CEO Atlanta Convention and Visitors Center, and former CMO, BellSouth Corporation

Lance Pierce CEO, NetHope and former President, Global

Development and Head of Partnerships and Sustainable Finance, ADEC Foundation

Amy Rapawy SVP, Marketing Centric Brands

Mollye Rhea President and Founder, For Momentum

Kirsten Suto Seckler Chief Marketing and Communications Officer, Shatterproof, former Chief Brand and Marketing Officer for Special Olympics

Mike Siegel former SVP, Marketing, St. Jude Children's Research Hospital

Ramesh Subramaniam former Partner, Consequent and former Head of Strategy and Marketing, Channels and Alliances, Equifax

Damon Taugher former VP Global Programs, Direct Relief

Jane Turner former Executive Director, Children's Museum of Atlanta

Tycely Williams CEO, Liberty Fellowship and former Chief Development Officer, Bipartisan Policy Center

ABOUT THE AUTHOR

Cynthia Currence has over 30 years experience working with non-profit organizations and a strong track record for creating powerful relationships that go well beyond the exchange of a "halo" effect for corporations and a "check" for nonprofits. The foundation of her success lies in investing time to understand the needs and requirements of internal and external audiences when co-creating shared value in business opportunities. This participatory approach to asset mapping is essential to the discovery of innovative solutions and significant bottom-line results for all partners and their beneficiaries. Her career accomplishments include:

- Generation of cause-marketing relationships ranging from $250,000 to $15 million with companies like Citibank, Glaxo Welcome, MetLIfe, General Mills, and Weight Watchers.

- Creation and management of business plans, teams, and support systems for the American Cancer Society's corporate engagement strategy designed to generate $100 million in annual cash and contributed services.

• Leadership of major gift operations for World Vision, Women for Women International, and Children International.

Cynthia worked with the American Cancer Society (ACS) for 18 years in senior positions, including VP of Strategic Corporate Marketing Alliances, VP of Strategic Marketing and Branding, and VP of International Marketing. Prior to working with the ACS, she spent 12 years with the United Way system, including an internal consultant role with United Way of America. She chaired two national American Marketing Association conferences focused on nonprofit marketing and served on the AMA Foundation Board of Trustees. She also served on the local and national boards for the Institute of Management Consultants and on the board of NetHope, an international membership organization of the largest international relief nonprofits that serve over a billion people. Cynthia has lectured internationally on brand and cause marketing.

www.ingramcontent.com/pod-product-compliance
Lightning Source LLC
Chambersburg PA
CBHW040918210326
41597CB00030B/5121